W9-CAI-524

WIRETAPPING ON TRIAL

A Case Study in the Judicial Process

STUDIES IN
POLITICAL SCIENCE

WIRETAPPING ON TRIAL

A Case Study in the Judicial Process

WALTER F. MURPHY
Princeton University

Random House New York

FIRST PRINTING

Library of Congress Catalog Card Number: 65-13762

MANUFACTURED IN THE UNITED STATES OF AMERICA

For Kelly and Holly

Preface

This book is designed to introduce beginning students to the mechanics of the judicial process, as well as to the policy-making role of judges in the American political system. While I have focused this work on the problem of wiretapping, I have not attempted to do an exhaustive study of that issue. Rather, I have tried to use wiretapping as a thread to trace some of the patterns in which administrative, legislative, and judicial officers interact to influence the development of public policy.

I am well aware of the limited value of the case approach as a means of deepening theoretical knowledge about political behavior.[1] I believe, however, that if it is competently done, a case study can be an effective teaching device, especially at the introductory level. And I have aimed this book at the student rather than at the expert.

I am indebted to many people for advice and help. The staffs of the Library of Congress and the Michigan Historical Collections at Ann Arbor were most kind in facilitating my use of the papers of Chief Justices William Howard Taft and Harlan Fiske Stone and of Justice Frank Murphy. My research assistants, Stephen Beckwith and Irving Faber, performed a number of necessary chores, searching for bibliographical material, checking footnotes, and discovering many tidbits of information. My friends and colleagues, William M. Beaney of Princeton and David Danelski of Yale, read the manuscript and not only saved me from many errors, but also helped me keep my objectives in perspective. Mrs. Helen Wright acted in her usual capacity as typist extraordinary and general editor. Last, my wife and children exhibited great patience in adjusting their lives to my writing.

Contents

WIRETAPPING ON TRIAL

A Case Study in the Judicial Process

CHAPTER

1

Introduction

It is now a commonplace among political scientists that courts are an integral part of the American governmental process. Two generations ago this sort of statement usually had a muckraking ring to it. In quiet, intellectual fashion able scholars like Edward S. Corwin and Robert E. Cushman tried to explain the inevitable involvement of judges in policy-making. More frequently, however, it was a strident cry from a disappointed litigant that linked the courts to the political process—and "political" in this context usually meant corruption, not policy-making.

Judges themselves did not help to clarify matters. More often than not they piously proclaimed that their function was only one of exercising judgment, not will, of merely declaring "the law." In later years many judges have dropped this mechanical explanation of their work and have come to realize and to admit in public that their task is far more complicated, involving as it does the perception and discretion of the statesman as well as the expertise of the legal craftsman. Judges' more realistic appraisal of their own work has been accompanied by—and is partially the result of—dispassionate analyses of judicial work by outside observers. So long, however, as courts decide cases of fundamental importance to American society, invective will constitute a large part of the literature on the judicial branch of government.

Thus it is important to keep in mind that to say that judges make law and so share in making policy does not imply that judges think and act just like legislators or administrators.[1] Judges cannot roam at will, looking for problems in need of solution. Courts are passive instruments of government in the sense that the problem must seek the judge, not the judge the problem. Once a case is brought before a court, the judge—or judges, if it is a collegial tribunal—can act only if the litigants meet certain technical requirements of jurisdiction and what is called "standing to sue."

When it is clear that the court can hear the case, the judge's decision will in part be shaped by previous decisions. There is a great deal of certainty in law, even constitutional law, though it is by no means the exact science many jurists used to pretend it was. *Stare decisis* —the following of previous decisions—cannot be an iron rule in a growing nation. No two situations are exactly alike. Time erodes the practicality of some doctrines and requires that they be revised or discarded. There must always be room for change and growth in the law, as in life itself. Nevertheless, judges generally try to follow the principles of earlier decisions. Where changes have to be made the courts, in the common law tradition, tend to make them slowly, adjusting gradually rather than reforming swiftly.

Judges are further inhibited by the kinds of action they can take. They are limited, first of all, by the requests made by the parties to a case. If, for instance, a U.S. Attorney comes into court and prosecutes a defendant for using the mails to defraud, the trial judge may not change the charge to smuggling. If a person goes into court and asks a judge to forbid a city official to interfere with a sit-in demonstration, the judge may not order the mayor to appoint a new police chief. Occasionally, an appellate court in reviewing a trial court decision may find an error of which neither party was aware, an error serious enough to require reversing the trial judge's decision or the jury's verdict. But, in the federal courts at least, such occasions are relatively infrequent.

Judges' actions are also limited by the remedies available to them. A court might hold that Congress cannot constitutionally enact a social security tax, but one judge, or even all judges, cannot themselves establish such a system or command members of Congress to do so. It must also be kept in mind that a court order binds only the parties to a case, their agents, employees, and associates, and, where public officials are involved, their successors in office. For instance, an order that Atlanta must desegregate its public schools does not legally bind officials of Augusta—though, of course, such an order is an excellent indication of what will happen if a Negro from Augusta decides to go to court to end segregated schools.

Judges are also limited by their conception of their office. Federal judges in particular have expressed awareness of their anomalous position as appointed officers possessing vast powers in a supposedly democratic nation. Most judges with a realistic notion of their function have tried not to second guess legislators and administrators as to what policy is wisest or best, but rather to decide only whether the particular official involved in a case had authority to act as he did. Yet anyone familiar with elementary psychology would expect that few men could ever completely detach themselves from their own preferences; and everyone familiar with American constitutional history knows that judges have often failed to carry into practice their ideals of self-restraint. On the other hand, it is equally apparent that judges have frequently attempted to exercise self-restraint and that such efforts can be a significant factor in inhibiting free judicial choice.

Judges are also subject to important political restraints. Each state has its own constitutional arrangements, sometimes including a requirement that judges be elected for relatively short terms. Federal judges are checked by a wide variety of limitations. Congress can enlarge or restrict the jurisdiction of courts, impeach and remove judges, pass new legislation changing judicial interpretations of the common law or of existing statutes, and propose constitutional amendments to thwart the policy effect of specific decisions or to alter the traditional role of the judiciary in American government. Moreover, federal judges are utterly dependent on congressional appropriations to pay their salaries and to meet the costs of operating their tribunals and executing their decisions.

Congress may also strike at one particular court, as legislators frequently have threatened to do in disputes with the Supreme Court. Increasing the number of justices—packing the Court—has been a recurring objective of elected politicians who have sharply disagreed with the justices' decisions. In addition, Congress may simply abolish one tier of federal courts, as the Jeffersonians did to the circuit courts in 1802; some Radical Republicans spoke of doing the same to the Supreme Court during the Civil War and Reconstruction.

The President in nominating judicial appointees and the Senate in confirming them can also help shape the role of the judiciary. As Chief Executive, the President commands the marshals who enforce court decisions. He can instruct them not to execute a court order and pardon them if they are convicted of contempt of court, just as he can pardon any person convicted of a federal crime. And as chief legislator and leader of his party, the President can use his influence to persuade Congress to employ any of the legislative checks on judicial authority.

Furthermore, there are important institutional limitations within the judicial system. Lower court judges are subject to review and reversal by appellate court judges. But this check is reciprocal; appellate court judges are also dependent on lower court judges to apply their rulings to specific cases. For instance, federal trial courts handle almost 100,000 cases a year. The Supreme Court can review less than a hundred of these if it is also to review cases coming from state courts. The Supreme Court justices must depend on the 350 federal judges—as well as on the thousands of state judges—to carry out Supreme Court policy, and it sometimes happens that lower court judges have ideas about law and policy that differ significantly from those of Supreme Court justices.

In addition, appellate courts are collegial tribunals. Any decision or formal opinion given in the name of the court must have the approval of a majority of the judges. Majority approval of a decision is not always as easy to obtain as it might seem at first glance, since often there are more than two alternatives. But arriving at a decision is comparatively simple when compared to the task of securing majority consent to a closely reasoned document phrased in terms of legal principles and vitally affecting public policy.

The power of judges is thus limited, but it is still great. Law, after all, is one of the chief vehicles for carrying public policy into effect, and as John Marshall remarked, "It is, emphatically, the province and duty of the judicial department to say what the law is."[2]

Three points are necessary to an understanding of the political—that is, policy-making—role of American courts. First, as J. W. Peltason has observed, judges make policy not as a matter of will but of function,[3] and this function is most visible at the Supreme Court level. No matter how the justices interpret the Constitution—whether they rule segregation valid or invalid, redistricting necessary or unnecessary, prayers in public schools permissible or impermissible—the justices will have vitally affected public policy in the entire nation, even though officials of only one school board, city, or state are immediately bound to obey the ruling.

Second, in deciding such cases judges often have room—indeed, need—for wide discretion. The words of some constitutional clauses are so vague, Felix Frankfurter once remarked, that they require a judge to interpret them by reading life itself rather than just esoteric legal documents. This statement is no less true of statutes and executive orders; and interpretations of statutes and executive orders may have effects comparable in scope and significance to interpretations of the Constitution.

Third, it must be kept in mind that while judges have leeway, they do not have complete freedom to let their personal preferences run wild—at least not without severe risk of being curbed.

This book is an illustration of the way the judicial process operates in conjunction with the legislative and executive processes in the formulation of public policy. The issue which forms the focus of investigation is wiretapping, and much of this study is devoted to a close analysis of one decision, *Olmstead* v. *United States*—its genesis, its unfolding, and its impact. No one can say that the Olmstead case is typical of the judicial process. There are too many cases, too many issues, too many judges to allow one to call any single case typical. But

Olmstead's problems with federal authorities do help illustrate how the judicial process frequently operates as a part of the more general process of public policy-making.

We will see federal executive officials take on themselves the task of carrying out a specific public policy. The courts will hold that policy legitimate, in spite of dissents from within the judicial and executive branches of government. Congress, after additional wrangling within the legislative and executive departments, will pass a new statute; and a fresh majority of judges will hold the old executive policy partially invalid. Some executive officials will return to Congress and ask for a modification of the new statute, meanwhile putting into practice variations on the old policy—variations that will meet with a partially favorable, partially hostile judicial reaction. And once again, some officials will return to the legislative forum.

This book records no final point in the wiretapping controversy, because the last word has not yet been spoken and probably will not be spoken so long as Americans cherish privacy but recognize a strong need for protection against criminals. The process of adjusting public policy to achieve, insofar as possible, both these values has been and is likely to remain continuous. In that process judges, as well as administrators and legislators, will play a prominent role.

CHAPTER

2

Prohibition

To many people prohibition was a noble experiment. To many others it was the greatest source of crime since a certain serpent tempted a well-known couple to try a fruit diet. To still other people—some of whom wore badges, some of whom did not—prohibition was no more than an opportunity to run a very lucrative business. To most Americans, however, prohibition was simply a nuisance. It had closed the saloon and opened the speakeasy, and in so doing raised the price and lowered the quality of available alcoholic beverages. At the same time the new social order added a sporting element to drinking; one could never be sure the liquor was not poisonous, though there was some comfort in the knowledge that this sort of poison was more apt to blind than to kill.

The politics of the adoption of the Eighteenth Amendment were a caricature of pressure group tactics as well as a frightening demonstration of popular apathy about public policy. The bulk of the American people, Frederick Lewis Allen has noted, accepted the proposed constitutional amendment "not only willingly, but almost absent-mindedly."[1] Docile acceptance may have been the public mood in January 1919 when the thirty-sixth state ratified the amendment, but one year later, when prohibition actually went into effect, most Americans had already made up their minds to temper their formal abstinence with informal drinking.

In the National Prohibition Act, more widely known as the Volstead Act, Congress attempted to set up machinery for rigid enforcement of the Eighteenth Amendment. As any detached and intelligent student of human nature—or police administration—could have predicted, the Volstead Act was doomed to failure. Even if the prohibition service had been honest and efficient, its task would have been formidable indeed. Twelve thousand miles of coast and almost seven thousand miles of land, river, and lake border presented an inviting and vulnerable target for smuggling liquor into the country. Thirst and American ingenuity soon made every house and apartment in the country a potential source of bathtub gin, or at least home-brewed beer.

Generally speaking, however, enforcement was neither honest nor efficient. Federal officers operated on a far higher plane than did most state officials, but the United States Bureau of Prohibition was riddled with corruption. Even President Warren G. Harding—a man not noted for being overly sensitive to graft—stated in a message to Congress that conditions of prohibition enforcement "savor of a nation-wide scandal." Still, it is difficult to determine whether the prohibition service would be more accurately described as dishonest or inefficient. For some years federal prohibition agents were not required to pass any sort of civil service examination and, once commissioned, they were given little specialized training for their work. When in 1927 Congress finally got around to requiring professional examinations for field agents, the results were disastrous. The Commissioner of Prohibition admitted that almost three-quarters of his men had failed the test.[2]

Many agents, state and federal, were, of course, honest and dedicated and, occasionally, well trained. These officers were undoubtedly among the most frustrated people of all history. Stymied by corrupt colleagues and superiors, often outmaneuvered by their antagonists the bootleggers, they were scorned and detested by the very citizens whose laws they were trying to enforce. Americans were determined to have whiskey and at the same time were prone to elect politicians pledged to maintain prohibition. To accommodate this contradictory behavior, most people were perfectly willing to bribe or condone the bribing of dishonest officials and to risk arrest by honest officials.

The telephone was a major instrument in bootlegging operations. Calls to Canada and Mexico set up smuggling expeditions into the United States. Calls to wholesale caches helped maintain the stock of speakeasies. Telephone calls expedited the business of those liquor dealers who specialized in home deliveries. Not least, the telephone was a quick and crucial means of warning bootleggers of impending police raids.

It must have been obvious to prohibition agents that if they could listen in on these conversations they could obtain a complete picture of a bootlegger's method of operating—the names and addresses of his suppliers, his customers, his employees, and even of his informants among the police. Eavesdropping, however, still had an unpleasant, even unethical connotation in American society. Ideally it was something a gentleman simply did not do, though it was also apparent that many gentlemen (and many more ladies) had frequent lapses in both their private and their official roles.

By the time of prohibition, nevertheless, electronic eavesdropping—wiretapping—was hardly a novel idea.

It had become so widespread that Congress had outlawed it during World War I; by the 1920s a number of states had laws permanently banning wiretapping, though most of these statutes were vague in coverage and represented more a carry-over from older legislation forbidding the pirating of telegraph messages than a deliberate and comprehensive effort to cope with the problems presented by the telephone.

The official policy of the United States government continued to be opposed to wiretapping. In 1924, when President Coolidge appointed his old college friend Harlan Fiske Stone Attorney General and commanded him to clean up the scandals in the Department of Justice which had festered under the Warren Harding–Harry Daugherty regime, Stone issued an order forbidding department officials to wiretap. This order, incidentally, had the strong support of a rising young Bureau of Investigation* official named J. Edgar Hoover. The Department of the Treasury, under which prohibition enforcement was then lodged, was also officially opposed to tapping telephone lines.

Policy-making in the executive branch of government, however, is rarely the product of a simple, hierarchical structure modeled on a military organization. A policy directive from Washington, D.C. may be only an entry in a filing cabinet in the U.S. Attorney's office in Tucson, Arizona. Bureaucracy, it has been noted, "more nearly resembles the arena of international politics than a group of disciplined subordinates responsible to the control of common superiors."[3]

Undoubtedly there were influential officers in the Treasury Department who were sufficiently embarrassed by the inefficiency of prohibition enforcement to wink at almost any means that would put bootleggers in jail and

* In 1935 the name of the Bureau of Investigation was changed to the Federal Bureau of Investigation.

get favorable publicity for the government's war against Demon Rum. The frustration and dedication of many honest prohibition agents probably made it inevitable that sooner or later some zealous officers would use wiretapping. And the dependence of bootleggers on the telephone made it very likely that the first wiretapping case would expose a sordid network of affluent businessmen, corrupt government officials, and petty criminals living off an unquenchable and illicit public thirst.

CHAPTER

3

The Olmstead Gang

On the afternoon of October 13, 1924, federal Prohibition Agent Earl Corwin and two assistants watched a pair of known bootleggers drive out of a Seattle garage. The officers got into their car and whipped off in pursuit. Since the bootleggers made no effort to escape, they were quickly overtaken. As the agents pulled up to the bootleggers' car, they caught a heavy smell of whiskey, but one of the bootleggers smiled and shook his head in mock sadness. "Why, Mr. Corwin, we haven't anything in the car; we have unloaded already."

"Unloaded what?" Corwin asked.

"We had a little load of liquor this morning," the bootlegger laughed, "but we got rid of it all."[1]

The agents took their prisoners back to the garage and went over the property with meticulous care. They found what their search warrant had specified they were looking for—illegal liquor, but only 30 cases. This was incriminating evidence, but it was hardly a big enough catch to worry a bootlegging ring of any size were it not for the fact that in the past few months federal agents had been making a series of harassing raids. When the boxes of contraband liquor were piled up, one of the bootleggers ventured a compliment: "You fellows will be getting the Big Boy himself one of these days, if you keep this up." When Corwin asked who was the "Big Boy," the bootlegger blandly replied: "Roy Olmstead, of course."

Al Capone's men also called their boss the "Big Boy," but, although Roy Olmstead ran the largest bootlegging operation in western Washington, he was no Alphonse Capone. In Seattle there were no gangland wars. Olmstead never resorted to killings or beatings or other forms of physical violence. He ran a quiet, profitable business, and he remained a quiet businessman, losing most of his dark hair, perhaps, but still rather dapper at thirty-eight. In 1920 he had been a lieutenant on the Seattle police force, but after pleading guilty to a charge of smuggling liquor he had been dismissed from his position. Once freed from official responsibilities, Olmstead was able to devote his full time to supplying the thirsty citizens of Seattle with liquid refreshment. With his connections in Seattle government, a small initial investment, and eleven partners (each of whom put up $1000 to Olmstead's $11,000; the profits were to be split in the same proportions), he was soon in charge of a prospering operation. Like President Harding, Roy Olmstead believed in less government in business, and more business in government.

As the captured bootlegger had suggested, prohibition agents were after the Big Boy. For some months now they had been secretly tapping his telephone lines—at his home and at his office—and later the telephones of some of his associates. What these agents were learning made Olmstead appear to be a very big boy indeed. His organization had some fifty employees—salesmen, telephone operators, watchmen, warehousemen, deliverymen, truck drivers, bookkeepers, a lawyer, and even an official fixer, though Olmstead himself remained on intimate terms with some of his old police colleagues. The liquor was brought from England to Vancouver in three small ocean-going freighters which Olmstead chartered. These ships would stay well outside of American territorial waters and would be met by one or more of Olmstead's three fast motorboats. The freighters, of course, could carry large quantities of whiskey, and each of the speedboats could haul over 700 cases.

Once ashore, the whiskey was stored at a ranch outside Seattle and at four distribution points (two garages, two paintshops) in town, and even occasionally at Olmstead's office. A small fleet of three trucks stood by to transport the liquor from the boats to the ranch or from the ranch to the distribution points. Deliveries to customers were made by four cars—one Cadillac and one Packard, plus two Fords for work in less affluent neighborhoods.

The list of customers was long and impressive. In addition to individuals, it included many of the better known hotels and restaurants in town, and even the local press club. The organization might move as many as 200 cases a day, and gross receipts usually ran between $150,000 and $200,000 a month, with a net profit of about $4,000 after expenses and protection had been paid. With his share of the proceeds Olmstead lived in the best section of town in a huge house which reporters were later to describe as "palatial." But he remained in most ways a humble, small businessman. He would sometimes answer the organization's phone and take orders, help wrap bottles, or make an actual delivery himself. Other than his home, Olmstead's only sign of conspicuous consumption was a radio station housed in his residence. In the evenings his wife amused herself by playing the piano and broadcasting bedtime stories—and in so doing managed to drive federal agents almost to distraction. They were certain that she was sending coded messages to the liquor ships; but if prohibition officers were ever able to discover such a code they made no public announcement about it.

After a customer telephoned Olmstead's office and placed an order, the organization's man would call one of the distribution points and tell a driver to make the delivery. By crossing Olmstead's telephone wires, federal agents could cause him or his men to misdial. The telephone operator would then come onto the line and ask what number had been dialed. The agents could thus get the number—and indirectly the address—of the distribution points.

It was through this tapping process that the raids during the late summer and early fall of 1924 were carried out. An experienced gangster might have been alarmed at the success of the prohibition agents in spotting distribution points, but Olmstead was sure he was safe. After all, relations with the Seattle police were pleasant, if expensive. He was tipped off by a police lieutenant whenever local officials planned a raid, and telephone conversations indicated that the mayor himself was cooperating with the organization. Indeed, Olmstead's friends in the city government were very apt to crack down hard on those drinking establishments which did not buy from the Big Boy.

When, in July, one of Olmstead's employees called to warn him that "the feds" were after him, the Big Boy calmly replied: "Well, they may just as well let down. They can't buck this gang." A few days later the employee called again to repeat his warning. This time Olmstead was less patient: "No, the city won't, and those other sons of bitches are too slow to catch cold."

By September, however, even a man as placid as Olmstead had to become suspicious about the preciseness of the prohibition agents' information. Several times he mentioned that he thought his telephone might be tapped, but he continued business as usual. Prohibition agents later remembered his telling them, after an unsuccessful raid on September 11, "There must be a leak somewhere. I wonder where it is? It may be one of my men, or it may be one of yours. I'd like to find out. I have been slipped up on several times lately." Still, on that occasion Olmstead maintained his outward calm and invited the agents to have breakfast with him, explaining that the load of liquor had by then been shunted off to another distribution point.

By November 1924 prohibition agents were ready to close their files on the Olmstead case. They planned a raid on his home in the hope of catching him with the physical evidence of his bootlegging operations—if not stores of liquor, at least bookkeeping records of his activities. On November 5 an informer called Olmstead to warn him. "Uncle is on your trail," the informer said, "and is going to stick this time." Even if Olmstead had taken this message more seriously than the earlier admonitions, it was too late; federal officers had a mass of wiretapping evidence to prove his command function.

At 9 o'clock on the evening of November 17, prohibition agents, armed with a search warrant, surrounded the Olmstead house. They quickly moved in, arresting Olmstead, his wife, and their guests. After a search of the premises uncovered no illegal liquor, the agents used Olmstead's telephone to call other members of his organization, asking them to come to the Olmstead house and bring some whiskey. In these conversations, one of the agents pretended to be Olmstead, and the officer's wife claimed to be Mrs. Olmstead. As the bootleggers arrived, they too were arrested and their liquor confiscated to be used in evidence against them. Sometime between 2:30 and 3:30 the next morning, after Olmstead's private papers had been found and seized (the warrant had stated that the thing sought was liquor, not papers, and a warrant gives lawful authority to seize only the objects specifically described), the whole group was taken to the U.S. district court and charged with violating the Volstead Act.

The next day, the Seattle newspapers carried banner headlines and front-page stories recounting the full story of the raid and arrests. The *Daily Times* dramatically reported that, "With search warrants, the federal agents last night swooped down upon the Olmstead home while sounds of merriment issued from the house, and a line of automobiles outside indicated a 'party' was in progress."[2] Before the afternoon papers were off the presses, however, Mr. and Mrs. Olmstead and most of their guests were back at their homes. Olmstead's lawyer, Jeremiah Finch, had gone to the federal courthouse and posted bail for them. Meanwhile, United States Attorney (the federal equivalent of a district attorney) Thomas P. Revelle, a former preacher who abhorred the use of intoxicating spirits, announced that he would convene a grand jury to consider the evidence against the Olmstead organization, but that because the evidence was so voluminous at least two weeks would be needed to put it into logical order for presentation.

On November 22, just five days after the Olmstead raid, prohibition agents raided the office of Jeremiah Finch. Again, although their warrant specified the items sought as certain bottles of illegal liquor, the agents seized only Finch's private papers—many of them correspondence with his client, Roy Olmstead. Before taking him to the courthouse and formally charging him with violating the Volstead Act, the officers thoughtfully gave Finch a receipt for his papers.

Despite the government's delay in obtaining an indictment, the Olmstead case stayed in the public spotlight.

Prohibition agents announced that these arrests represented only the opening gun in a major war against liquor traffic on the West Coast. On the other hand, almost immediately after the arrests, the mayor had unleashed an attack on the prohibition officers for trying a "grandstand play." "I don't hold any brief for Olmstead," the mayor stated, "but they didn't have to go about it in that way. The federal agents have a standing invitation from me to help clean up the bootleggers, but will never work with me."[3]

In reply, Roy C. Lyle, head of the local office of the prohibition force, said only:

> The raid on Monday night was only an incident to work that we have been doing for months. We hoped to get some of his [Olmstead's] henchmen coming to confer with him, but in answer to telephone calls, the majority of them sent subordinates. However, we have a mass of real evidence. We will leave it to the federal court to answer whether or not it is a grandstand play.[4]

Unimpressed with this reply—and perhaps a bit wary that federal officers were suspicious of him—the mayor repeated his blast at prohibition agents, claiming that they were not uniformly enforcing the Volstead Act and were trying to hide their failure to keep liquor out of the country by inflating petty arrests into sensational coups. The Seattle police, he proudly asserted, had made more arrests and secured more convictions than had federal and county authorities put together. The mayor closed with a challenge:

> Now Mr. Lyle, Hazeltine, Whitney, *et al.*, show your figures and let's have an accounting. Your people and [the] Pope may grandstand a credulous Christian public, but you cannot retain your

> standing if your actual performance is compared with the work of real men. I defy you to produce the figures.[5]

Unable to answer the mayor without exposing more of their case against Olmstead and his associates than they felt was tactically wise, prohibition agents avoided further public controversy with city officials, at least for the time being. Lyle merely noted that Olmstead, although masterminding bootlegging in western Washington, was only one member of a huge organization and that other officers in his group would also be caught and prosecuted.

While the citizens of Seattle waited—with mixed emotions, one suspects—for the promised new arrests, the mayor began to have troubles of a different sort. On November 24 the City Council's Efficiency Committee heard testimony that a firm had lost a $1,250,000 tunnel construction contract because it had refused to hire the mayor's son.[6]

On January 19, 1925 Olmstead and his associates—and perhaps many of his customers—received a collective jolt when a federal grand jury indicted more than 90 persons for violating and conspiring to violate the Volstead Act and applicable tariff regulations. The principal persons accused were Olmstead, his wife, and his lawyer, Jeremiah Finch.

An indictment is a formal accusation that a person or group of persons has committed a crime. The Constitution requires that in cases involving a "capital or otherwise infamous crime"—that is, felonies, crimes for which the punishment could exceed one year's imprisonment—a defendant can be tried in a federal court only after being indicted by grand jury. (Most states, on the other hand, have been moving toward a system whereby a prosecutor formally accuses a defendant simply by filing a document known as "information" with a court of competent jurisdiction. This information, like an indictment, tells the judge that a crime has been committed and asks that the defendant named be brought to trial.)

The grand jury is usually composed of sixteen to twenty-three men and women summoned at regular intervals or on special occasions to hear evidence of crimes committed within the jurisdiction of a federal district court. Although legally competent to conduct its own investigations and subpoena witnesses, federal grand juries today normally hear only the evidence the prosecutor puts before them. Proceedings before a grand jury do not constitute a trial. The suspect may or may not be called as a witness; the jury does not pass on his guilt or innocence, but only on the question whether he should be made to stand trial. If a majority or more of the jurors find sufficient evidence to accuse a person of a criminal act, they return an indictment, or "true bill." If the jurors find the evidence insufficient to accuse, they return a "no bill." All proceedings before the grand jury are secret, and disclosure by any person—witness, prosecutor, or juror—of what transpired is a criminal offense.

Included in the indictment in the Olmstead case were two Seattle policemen. They were accused of conspiring to aid Olmstead in violating the liquor and tariff laws. The mayor, of course, was outraged. He charged that the entire Olmstead case was based on "backyard washday gossip," and revoked the suspensions the police chief had placed on the accused officers. "There is a handful of policemen," the mayor asserted, "who want to undermine me so they can get more lucrative positions, but they couldn't get the mayor—not the mayor—so they struck at those near to the mayor."[7] Prohibition officers, he continued, were conspiring with these disgruntled policemen and even had him under surveillance. The mayor vowed to write directly to Washington and have the agents fired.

The mayor was whistling in the dark, and he knew it. The wiretapping had been an official secret, but stories were now leaking out that the case against the Olmstead organization was built around evidence obtained through monitored telephone calls. When pressed by reporters, Revelle, the U.S. Attorney, admitted that he had heard such rumors but said he "understood" that federal officers had not engaged in wiretapping activities. Meanwhile, he promised an early trial for the defendants, though he could see no prospect of beginning before June.

As it turned out, Revelle's prediction of June was far too optimistic. The docket of the local federal district court was crowded with cases, and the Olmstead litigation was already threatening to be long and complex as the defendants began a series of time-consuming legal maneuvers to escape the trap in which they had been caught.

On April 6, thirty-three of the defendants appeared in the United States District Court for the Western District of Washington and entered a plea in abatement. This is a technical motion by the defense which attacks not the merits of the opposing side's allegations, but the time or manner in which those allegations are made. Here the defendants asserted that the indictment was so defective that they could not be made to stand trial. The defendants were represented by three counsel. Jeremiah Finch ignored the old lawyer's maxim that the attorney who defends himself has a fool for a client, and appeared for himself, Mr. and Mrs. Olmstead, and twenty-three others. The remainder of the accused employed two counsel of their own choosing.

By this time, the defendants were not only aware that wiretapping had been used to gather evidence against them; they also knew many of the details of how the taps had been conducted. Undoubtedly they had guessed some of the story from the grand jury proceedings. In addition, one of the wiretappers, an unsavory character who had demanded his pay from the government in whiskey, had left federal service after a quarrel over wages and was freely talking about his police activities. Using this information, the defendants' lawyers contended that the indictment was defective for three reasons.

First they asserted that the indictment had been based on wiretap evidence, and this sort of evidence was "incompetent, irrelevant, hearsay, and secondary testimony" because the persons who listened had merely scribbled longhand notes, which were later edited and typed by another person or persons and material added and subtracted. Thus the wiretap "evidence" presented to the grand jury was not a verbatim account supplied by the actual eavesdroppers but a doctored and unreliable second-hand version of what had been overheard.

Second, the defendants charged that a federal prohibition agent had pressured a member of the grand jury into voting for an indictment rather than a no bill. When the grand jury was in session, they alleged, Agent William M. Whitney, who had prepared the list of names of those whom the government thought should be indicted, called the foreman of the jury out of the room and told him that the wiretaps showed he had been a customer of Olmstead. According to the defendants, Whitney said that if the grand jury returned a no bill, another jury would be convened and the foreman's name added to the government's list. Within two hours of this conversation the grand jury returned the indictment.

Third, counsel argued that the searches of Olmstead's house and Finch's office were illegal in that agents had not shown the "probable cause" which the Constitution requires for the issuance of a search warrant. Moreover, when they had found no liquor, the agents had seized everything they thought might possibly help build a case—a "fishing expedition" in direct contravention of the Fourth Amendment's requirement that the place to be searched and the articles sought be specifically identified in the warrant.*

The U.S. Attorney, of course, opposed granting the plea and filed a motion "to strike," that is, to dismiss, the plea in abatement. U.S. District Judge Jeremiah Neterer took the arguments under consideration for two weeks, then granted the government's motion to strike. In a carefully worded opinion,† he stressed that the inherent secrecy of the grand jury proceedings precluded the judge from investigating the nature of the evidence the grand jury had weighed. The law established a presumption that the jurors, as sworn officers of the court,

* The Fourth Amendment reads: "The right of the people to be secure in their persons, houses, papers, and effects, against unreasonable searches and seizures, shall not be violated, and no Warrants shall issue, but upon probable cause, supported by Oath or affirmation, and particularly describing the place to be searched, and the persons or things to be seized."

† *United States* v. *Olmstead*, 7 F. 2d 756 (1925). The case title indicates that the federal government is prosecuting or suing Olmstead—*United States* v. *Olmstead*. (The names of other defendants are usually omitted or lumped under *et al.*) The citation is to the Federal Reporter, now in its second series. Seven designates the volume, and 756 the page in that volume at which the case begins. Thus the citation is to a case in volume 7, page 756 of the second series of the Federal Reporter, a case decided in 1925. This set of reports is published by the West Publishing Company, a private company in Minneapolis. Starting in 1930, the West Company began publishing only opinions of U.S. circuit courts of appeals in the Federal Reporter, and instituted a new set of volumes, the Federal Supplement (abbreviated F. Supp.), for district court opinions. As a commercial rather than a governmental enterprise,

would consider only proper evidence and nothing short of a demonstration that the jury had been illegally empanelled or had been guilty of fraud or misconduct could justify an investigation of its proceedings.

If, Judge Neterer continued, it were true that an agent had attempted to influence the foreman of the jury, the agent should be prosecuted for a criminal act. But the grand jury had decided on an indictment by a majority vote, with the foreman having only one vote, and there was no allegation that he had tried to sway any other juror. The foreman's special duty was only to sign the indictment if twelve of the twenty-three jurors voted for it, and this he had done.

Undeterred by this initial defeat, the defendants in early May filed a demurrer to the indictment. A demurrer (pronounced de-MER-rer) is a plea that whether or not a defendant has committed the acts with which he is charged, these acts are insufficient to constitute an offense under law. To support their plea, defense attorneys argued that the charges against their clients did not set forth the kind of facts necessary to show that a crime had been committed; no particular parts of these statutes were claimed to have been violated; nor did the alleged facts mention any specific action that could be criminal. Thus, each defendant asserted, every one of the counts was "so vague, indefinite and uncertain that it does not fairly or sufficiently inform this defendant of the charge he is expected to meet at the trial." Furthermore, the defense contended that it was improper in

---

the West Company feels it can profitably publish only a small number of the almost 100,000 cases handled each year by U.S. district courts and relies on federal judges to send the company the opinions they think worthy of general notice. Actually, this opinion by Judge Neterer was not published until after his opinion in a later stage in the pretrial proceedings, when it became apparent to the Judge as well as to West Company editors that the Olmstead case was going to become a landmark in American law.

terms of federal procedure for counts under the Volstead Act to be coupled with counts under the tariff statute.

Once again Judge Neterer ruled against the defendants. In another careful opinion, he conceded that the indictment was indeed prolix, but the law did not demand literary elegance. "The true test of the sufficiency of the allegations of an indictment is not whether it might have been made more certain, but whether it contains every element of the offense and sufficiently apprises the defendant of the charge to be met. . . ." This particular indictment, for all its verbosity, passed the relevant test. It charged a conspiracy, and the law did not require that an overt act be committed for a criminal conspiracy to exist and be punished. It was enough that such a conspiracy had been formed.

The judge also rejected the argument that accusations under prohibition and tariff statutes could not be combined. "The conspiracy charged in each count is a distinct offense, and belongs to the same class of crimes, and under the statute may be joined."

Battered but still not beaten, the defendants returned to Judge Neterer twelve days later and asked that he order the government to file a "bill of particulars"—a detailed answer to questions relating to the specific offenses with which each defendant was charged—so that they might be better prepared to defend themselves at the trial. Defense counsel filed forty-two questions, but the judge ordered the government to answer only ten of them.

With these preliminaries taken care of, Mr. and Mrs. Olmstead, Finch, and most of the other defendants came to the court on May 25, 1925 and formally entered pleas of not guilty. Several of the defendants, however, pleaded guilty. One of these was John McClean, whose job in the Olmstead organization had been to take telephone orders. In exchange for the U.S. Attorney's promise not to prosecute him, McClean promised to be a star witness for the government at the trial.

Still the case was not yet ready to go to trial. During the summer, Olmstead and Finch requested the judge to quash, or nullify, the warrants federal officers had used to enter Olmstead's home and Finch's office. The defendants claimed that the warrants had been issued without "probable cause" and that the search of Finch's office and the seizure of papers relating to Olmstead's activities constituted an infringement of the Fourth Amendment as well as of the confidential nature of the attorney–client relationship. Second, the defendants asked that the property seized in these illegal searches be returned. In addition, Olmstead and Finch asked the judge to refuse to allow the government to use any evidence obtained through wiretapping, because wiretapping abridged the Fourth Amendment's protection of privacy and the Fifth Amendment's protection against self-incrimination. Moreover, insofar as conversations between Finch and Olmstead had been monitored, the wiretapping had interfered with the confidence of the attorney–client relationship.

On September 21, 1925, Judge Neterer issued his ruling, denying in part and granting in part the motions to quash. Neterer found that federal agents had shown probable cause and thus that the warrants had been properly issued. However, the warrants had specified the objects to be seized as bottles of illegal liquor. The agents, therefore, had had no authority to take Olmstead's papers, and these documents could not be used against him. Nor could Finch's papers be used against him. Whether Finch's papers could be used against Olmstead would have to be determined at the trial when the government tried to introduce particular documents in evidence. Since constitutional rights were personal rights, these documents might be used against defendants other than Olmstead and Finch if relevancy were shown.

The judge then denied the motion to suppress wiretapping evidence:

> Wiretapping is not a national offense, nor made so by the statutes of the state of Washington [the judge was in error; wiretapping was a crime in Washington]; even so, it would not violate any constitutional right of the defendants to receive the testimony. The conversation is not a property right. If, as stated, the defendants Finch, Olmstead, with others, were conspiring to violate the laws of the United States, they could not seek protection under the confidential relation status. If the conversation referred to had been carried on in the home of the defendant Olmstead, between him and his attorney, and the conversation had been overheard by trespassers upon the premises, it would be competent testimony in support of the criminal charge. I know of no rule of law or evidence which would exclude it, and no decision which, even by inference, sustains the contention of the defendant.[8]

There was one more dilatory move. In November 1925, Olmstead and Finch petitioned for separate trials. Neterer rejected their requests on January 11, 1926. Finally, on the morning of January 19, 1926, exactly one year after the indictment had been returned and fourteen months after the raid on Olmstead's house, the clerk of the United States District Court for the Western District of Washington read the docket for the day: The United States of America versus Roy Olmstead, Elsie Olmstead, Jeremiah Finch, and numerous others.

CHAPTER

4

The Trial

Anticipating that the publicity which had attached to the Olmstead case would bring large crowds to the courtroom, the presiding judge had ordered federal marshals to keep out spectators until the defendants, their attorneys, government officials, members of the jury panel, and newspapermen had found chairs. The judge, it happened, had acted most prudently. Although it was a rainy winter day in Seattle, there was a huge turnout of curious citizenry who wanted to see the spectacle of a federal trial for violations of the liquor laws, and the "official guests" required most of the available 250 seats.

The forty-seven defendants—by now eight had pleaded guilty, three had fled, and the government had dropped charges against or postponed the trial of the rest—gathered together outside the courtroom. Promptly at 10 A.M. Jeremiah Finch, hat tilted back on his head, a long black cigar in his mouth, marched into the courtroom. Behind him came most of the other defendants and their attorneys. Then the U.S. Attorney and his assistants entered. A conscientious reporter tried to re-create the scene for his readers:

> For a few moments the crowd, forced to silence by the bailiff and marshals, looked out the high windows across a court at the rainwashed roof of another wing of the building, scrutinized the green walls and creamed ceiling with its rectangle of electric lights, rimming a smaller oval of globes. The polished desks for attorneys, the broad bench and desk of the judge with its corner posts of green-shaded lamps, and wicker backed jury box chairs, with their shiny polished frames, also were under careful observance.[1]

As the bailiff banged his gavel to order all present to stand for the entrance of Judge Neterer, Roy Olmstead and his wife walked into the back of the courtroom and most of the spectators swiftly turned to catch a glimpse of the Big Boy himself. Olmstead diverted the attention of the crowd from the judge's entrance, but it was to be the last scene he stole from Neterer.

Jeremiah Neterer was a quick, efficient jurist. Patient but stern, he rarely used his gavel—a sharp word or a cutting look was usually enough to quiet an overly contentious lawyer. Born in Goshen, Indiana, a small town not far from South Bend, Neterer had moved to Bellingham, Washington, as a twenty-eight-year-old lawyer. There he had taken an active part in local Democratic politics, had served for a short time as a judge of the superior court of Whatcom County, and had been appointed a federal district judge by Woodrow Wilson in 1913. At sixty-four, Neterer's hair was still as black as the horn-rimmed glasses he wore.

As soon as the judge seated himself, Finch began protesting that the widespread publicity surrounding the case was going to make it impossible to find twelve men whom biased newspaper stories had not already convinced that the defendants were guilty. Neterer cut him off with a remark that he found the newspaper reports sympathetic, not hostile, to the defendants.

After this opening plea, Finch played a minor role in the trial. A number of the defendants had retained George W. Vandeveer as their attorney, and he dominated the defense. Vandeveer was a former prosecutor with a finely honed skill in appealing to jurors' emotions; he was also a quick-tempered man equally at home in a street brawl or a courtroom debate. As a young lawyer (he was now fifty-one), he was apparently on his way to a brilliant career, but his life had been marred by a series of personal tragedies brought on in part by his political naïveté and his inability to handle money. His mistress had just committed suicide, and to overcome his grief Vandeveer threw himself into the Olmstead battle with all the energy and shrewdness that had earned him the title of "Clarence Darrow of the West."[2]

The first problem of the trial was to select a jury from the panel chosen at random—as the grand jurymen had been—from the territory within the court's jurisdiction. Each side may question every prospective juror, or venireman as he is technically called, to find out if he is prejudiced for or against the defendant, is associated socially or economically with either party to the case, or has already made up his mind about the proper outcome of the trial. Both the defense and the prosecution have an unlimited number of "challenges for cause"; that is, if either lawyer can demonstrate to the judge that a venireman is prejudiced or should be disqualified for some other reason, the judge will strike that venireman's name from the jury list. Ideally, a juror would have no knowledge of the case other than the evidence presented at the trial itself, but in a small community or even in an urban area with mass media of communication such selective ignorance is rare indeed. Accepting the realities of life, judges have refused to disqualify a juror for a "light opinion"—an inclination toward one side or the other, but one that the juror avows can be overcome by evidence to the contrary.

Every trial lawyer, however, sometimes intuitively senses that a prospective juror is basically hostile to his client or to the kind of claim his client is asserting. Recognizing the wisdom of this sort of intuition, state and federal statutes allow each side a limited number of what are called "peremptory challenges." Without giving a reason, each side may in effect order a specified number of veniremen to be dismissed from the panel. In the federal courts, the defense may make ten such challenges and the prosecution six in a criminal case involving a felony.

Delicate skill is required to question a prospective juror so as to bring out any latent prejudice without at the same time creating resentment and hostility, and lawyers usually go about practicing this occult art at their own pace. Moreover, when one side challenges a venireman for cause, the other may object that only good judgment, not prejudice, has been evidenced. Finch and Vandeveer got into a long series of wrangles with U.S. Attorney Thomas Revelle over challenging veniremen, and when the court adjourned after the first day's work only three jurors had been agreed upon. It was not until the end of the second day that opposing counsel could agree on a full panel of twelve, plus two alternates who would sit with the jury and take over if one or two jurymen became ill.

The twelve jurors were all men, and as jury panels go this one was probably better qualified intellectually than most to understand the legal arguments, gauge the probity of witnesses, and so decide the guilt or innocence of the defendants. The foreman, elected by the jurors themselves, was the vice president of a Seattle bank. Another member was president of a local department store, and four others were also business executives. Of the remaining six, two were farmers, one a rancher, another a lumberman, and another a mechanic. The last juror was H. G. York, a white-mustached, eighty-five-year-old retired businessman. York needed a cane to help him walk, but he was still mentally alert. Whenever a matter was being discussed that he did not understand, he would promptly interrupt and ask the judge for an explanation, the only juror who availed himself of this privilege.

As soon as the jurors had been selected, they were marched off under guard to a nearby hotel. They would stay there when court was not actually in session, protected as much as possible from contact with the outside world until they had arrived at a verdict or had been dismissed. Each morning the bailiff would march them, two by two, back to the courtroom. The judge opened their mail to make certain that no one was writing to them about the case, and the bailiff performed the nightly duty of telephoning wives to assure them that their husbands were in good health and were being well taken care of. After their incarceration had gone on for two weeks, the bailiff took pity on his charges and allowed them to go—under guard, of course—to see a play at a local theater.

On the morning of the third day the trial began in earnest. Each side made a brief opening statement to the jury, outlining what would or would not be proved. Then the prosecution began calling its witnesses. In all, fifty persons testified for the government and seventy-five for the defense.[3] Among the early witnesses were a boat builder who identified Olmstead as the man for whom he had constructed a speedboat and two Canadian officials who testified that Olmstead had tried to arrange permission for his boats to land in Canada without reporting to customs. Particularly damaging was the testimony of John McClean, the defendant who had pleaded guilty. McClean sketched in detail the origin of the Olmstead gang, the structure of the organization, its method of operation, and his own part in its functioning.

As the witnesses droned on, Judge Neterer rocked back and forth in his chair. Since it needed oil, it squeaked incessantly, but even this grating noise was not sufficient to prevent some of the defendants from falling asleep. Many members of the lower echelon of the Olmstead organization found the trial as dull as its maneuvers were incomprehensible. Especially during the afternoons, the marshals were kept busy shaking various defendants and warning them—with no apparent success—against napping in court. Revelle contributed to the somnolent atmosphere by asking long, drawn-out questions in a steady monotone, sounding, one newsman observed, "like a college professor."

Olmstead generally remained impassive but alert. As witnesses pointed him out he would, so a reporter at the trial wrote, smile "slightly, almost sarcastically," and look unflinchingly at those witnesses who walked across the floor and touched his shoulder to complete their identification. Olmstead, the *Seattle Daily Times* noted, was "bland and urbane, the type of man whose face always retains its youthful rotundity and a freshness sometimes called cherubic."[4]

Mrs. Olmstead was less calm. A woman well but simply dressed, she, like most of the defendants, appeared bored by the proceedings. Unlike her husband, she showed great nervousness during the early stages of the trial, twisting and knotting a handkerchief. But as the trial went on, she took to knitting, and the steady click of her needles became an accepted part of the courtroom scene.

Even the imaginative rewrite men in the editorial offices of the Seattle newspapers had been unable to generate much that was colorful or exciting about the first week of the trial. But on Monday, January 25, the dullness of the preceding days was smashed as federal Prohibition Agent William M. Whitney took the stand and began to testify about the evidence the government had obtained through wiretapping.

Vandeveer was immediately on his feet, protesting vehemently that use of such evidence violated the defendants' constitutional rights. Revelle replied in equally emotional tones that wiretap evidence was admissible. Essentially the defense attorneys made two points, and made them often and with increasing bitterness during the following weeks. First, they claimed that wiretapping violated the Fourth and Fifth Amendments to the Constitution. This much they had argued before the trial began, but now they added that wiretapping was illegal under state law in Washington. Thus, since the evidence was obtained in an unconstitutional and illegal manner, it could not be used in a federal court. As he had in the pretrial proceedings, Judge Neterer ruled against this objection each time it was raised.

The second defense objection related to the way in which the government witnesses presented the wiretap evidence.* The eavesdroppers had jotted down cryptic longhand notes as they listened to telephone conversations and, shortly afterward, had dictated more coherent statements to Mrs. Clara Whitney, William Whitney's wife. Mrs. Whitney transcribed these notes in shorthand and later typed them. Some months later, prohibition

* As the discussion grew more heated—and the judge continually ruled against them—defense counsel added a third argument: the Eighteenth Amendment to the Constitution had not been legitimately adopted because it had failed to receive the necessary two-thirds vote in Congress. Needless to say, the judge gave this point short shrift.

agents and the staff of the U.S. Attorney's office arranged the typewritten statements in a large black book of 775 pages. The original notes were then destroyed, and, Mr. Whitney admitted, the book itself was taken apart, rearranged, and rebound at least once.

Because there was no way anyone could test the veracity of Mrs. Whitney's shorthand notes and because the book had admittedly been edited, the defense argued that prosecution witnesses should not be allowed to use the book during their testimony at the trial.

Use of the book was vital to the prosecution. Since in this case alone prohibition agents had listened to thousands of telephone conversations they could offer only general recollections; without some memory aid it was not likely that they could recall specific statements overheard fifteen to nineteen months earlier. Revelle had planned that each of the eavesdroppers who testified would have a copy of the book on his lap, and whoever from the U.S. Attorney's staff was asking the questions would also have a copy. Thus the witnesses could respond to questions about particular conversations on given days.

The judge recognized the importance of the use or non-use of the book—the "Black Book," as the press quickly dubbed it—and allowed counsel for the defense and the government to argue the point for several hours. Then Neterer made his ruling: if an eavesdropper claimed an independent recollection of events about which he was testifying, he would be allowed to use the book to refresh his memory; but he would not be permitted to read from the book.

Defense counsel were understandably irritated at the ruling, and tempers flared. Revelle smiled broadly when Neterer announced his decision, and Vandeveer requested the judge to order the prosecution to stop laughing. Neterer reminded both sides that a trial was serious business. Revelle protested that sometimes he simply could not help smiling, and Vandeveer returned to the attack: "I suggest that he take his smiles home and not bring them around when men's liberties are at stake."[5]

"Proceed!" Neterer snapped.

The lawyers did proceed. They proceeded to wrangle angrily, as the defense fought doggedly to undermine the credibility of the wiretap evidence. To do so, defense attorneys demanded to have a copy of the Black Book so that they could cross-examine government witnesses. The judge at first refused this request; then, after another extended argument, he ruled that all pages of the book would be sealed except those to which prosecution witnesses referred in their testimony. The defense could examine the unsealed pages and those pages only.

This solution did not end the matter. When Revelle finished his direct examination of Whitney, Vandeveer asked the court for a recess before beginning his cross-examination so that he and his associates might carefully go over the Black Book. The prosecution had had the volume for over a year, and Revelle was very familiar with its contents. The defense attorneys had just been handed the book in the courtroom and had had only a few minutes to glance at the 470 pages referred to in Whitney's testimony. Neterer, however, denied the request, and the trial immediately continued.

Vandeveer kept questioning whether Whitney and the eavesdroppers who followed him did in fact have an independent recollection of particular conversations they had allegedly overheard. When Revelle was conducting his direct examination, Vandeveer and Finch had interrupted several times to complain that the witness was reading from the book. It was on cross-examination, however, that Vandeveer made his most telling points. He subjected the second eavesdropper-witness, Agent Richard L. Fryant, to a devastating series of inquiries, putting question after question to him about conversations he had discussed on direct examination; but without looking at his copy of the Black Book, the witness was unable to say a single word beyond "I don't know."

The substance of the eavesdroppers' testimony was the full story of the operations of the Olmstead organization: telephoned instructions about ship arrivals and rendezvous in Puget Sound, wholesale shipments from the cache at the ranch outside of town to distribution points within Seattle, retail orders from customers in town, information about cooperation by and/or payments to city officials ranging from motorcycle policemen to the mayor's office.

When the federal agents who had done the wiretapping completed their testimony, other prohibition officials took the stand and recounted what they had seen and heard in staking out and raiding Olmstead's distribution points. They claimed that Olmstead and some of his employees had freely admitted that they were in the bootlegging business. In addition, the steward of a Seattle night club testified that he had been a customer of Olmstead and identified some of the other defendants as the people who had delivered liquor to his establishment.

On February 9, after seventeen days of testimony, the prosecution rested its case, and once more Finch and Vandeveer moved that the wiretap evidence be excluded and the jury instructed to disregard it. Once more Judge Neterer denied the motion.

The next morning the defense began its case, and for the next nine days a parade of witnesses appeared. Finch took the stand and tried to show that he was only Olmstead's lawyer and had no connection with any possible conspiracy to violate the National Prohibition Act. More specifically he denied that he had tried to bribe a federal officer, as the officer had earlier testified. Elsie Olmstead also appeared as a witness and described the November 17, 1924 raid on her home. She accused prohibition agents of threatening to strike her when she tried to prevent their impersonating her on the telephone.

A former prohibition agent was called and testified that he had been one of the eavesdroppers. He claimed, contrary to what the other eavesdroppers had said, that during the taps they had frequently been unable to recognize the voices of those speaking and had later interpolated names when editing their notes. A stream of character witnesses testified about the reputations, good and bad, of earlier witnesses. Olmstead himself did not take the stand, possibly because he did not want to give the prosecution an opportunity to bring out on cross-examination that six years earlier he had been dismissed from the Seattle police force after being caught smuggling liquor into the United States.

When the testimony had been concluded, counsel for each side made closing statements to the jury. Revelle claimed to have proved beyond a reasonable doubt that the defendants had conspired together to operate a bootlegging ring. Defense attorneys again attacked the credibility of prosecution witnesses and the use of wiretapping. If Olmstead and the others were convicted, Vandeveer asserted, no man's privacy would be safe. He urged the jury to return a verdict of not guilty to prove that the community's standards of decency would not tolerate criminal activity by officers sworn to uphold the sanctity of the law.

Judge Neterer then gave his instructions to the jury. He began by noting that at the beginning of the trial the government had chosen to prosecute only on those counts involving the Volstead Act; therefore no charge of smuggling was before the court. Next the judge summed up the evidence, reminding the jurors three separate and distinct times that they were the sole judge of the facts in the case and that they should reject his summation if it did not comport with their own recollections or evaluations. The judge then pointed out that testimony for the prosecution by the defendant who had pleaded guilty should be scrutinized with extreme care since it came from a "polluted source." By this, he meant that this particular defendant may have testified as he did to win favor with the U.S. Attorney and thereby mitigate or possibly even escape punishment. However, Neterer continued, the jurors had seen the witness on the stand and heard his testimony. If they believed he spoke the truth, then a conspiracy would be established, at least among those defendants the witness had named.

In regard to Finch, the judge reminded the jury that it was absolutely proper for an attorney to represent persons accused of any crime whatever. Only if the jurors believed the testimony of the government agent that Finch had attempted to bribe him to stay away from the Olmstead organization could Finch be included in the conspiracy. Neterer also reminded the jurors that they could draw no inference of guilt from the fact that some of the defendants had not testified on their own behalf. The burden of proof was on the government, not on the defendants. The judge frankly stated that he believed the government had met that burden insofar as Olmstead and some of the other defendants were concerned, but again, Neterer reminded the jurors that his opinion on the facts was not binding on them.

The jurors could not vote to convict, the judge continued, unless they were convinced beyond a reasonable doubt that the government had proved the guilt of the defendants. "A reasonable doubt," he explained,

> is just such a doubt as the term implies; a doubt for which you can give a reason. It must not arise from a merciful disposition or kindly, sympathetic

> feeling or desiring to avoid a possibly disagreeable duty. It must be a substantial doubt such as an honest, sensible, fair-minded man might with reason entertain consistently with a conscientious desire to ascertain the truth and perform a duty. . . . It is just such a doubt as a man of ordinary prudence, sensibility, and decision, in determining an issue of like concern to himself as that before the jury to the defendant, would make him pause or hesitate in arriving at his conclusion. It is a doubt which is created by the want of evidence, or maybe by the evidence itself; not speculative, imaginary, or conjectural.

Finally, Neterer came to the wiretapping problem:

> This, Gentlemen of the Jury, is no place to punish anybody for wire-tapping, if offense has been committed. There is no law of the United States against it. If there is a law of the state and the parties have transgressed the law, then they should be punished as the law provides; the jurors should not violate their oaths as jurors of administering justice in this court as a penalty that should be administered elsewhere; I am satisfied that you will not give any thought to anything of that kind, but will determine this case solely upon the evidence presented here.

It was 9:30 on Friday evening, February 19, 1926, when the judge completed his instructions. The jury then retired to consider the case in secret. At midnight the foreman called the bailiff and told him that the jury would adjourn for the night. The bailiff then escorted them back to their hotel. At 8:40 the next morning he marched them back to court to resume their deliberations. As the hours dragged on, speculation began to grow that the jury was "hung"—unable to arrive at the required unanimous vote for any verdict—and a mistrial would have to be declared. Revelle told reporters that if such were the result, a new trial would begin in two weeks.*

This speculation proved groundless, however. At 2:10 that afternoon, the foreman opened the door of the jury room and called the marshal of the court over to inform him that a verdict had been reached. The marshal immediately told the judge and the U.S. Attorney and summoned the defendants and their lawyers.

Within an hour the *dramatis personae* and 150 spectators had assembled in the hushed courtroom. The defendants were tensely waiting to know whether they would go to prison or leave the building free men. Judge Neterer, his nerves worn thin by the incessant squabbling at the trial, was impatient to end this particular case and to move on to the other items on his steadily growing docket. As the judge took his seat, the bailiff called the roll of the jury, then asked: "Have you arrived at a verdict?"

"We have," the foreman replied and handed the bailiff a slip of paper. The bailiff started to bring the paper over to the judge, but Neterer asked him to read it aloud.

"In the District Court, United States versus Roy Olmstead—" the bailiff began.

"Never mind all that," Neterer interrupted.

"We the jury," the bailiff continued, "in the above entitled case find the defendant Roy Olmstead"—he stuttered at the name Olmstead—"is guilty as charged."

The bailiff then read the verdicts for the other defendants. Finch and nineteen others were found guilty; Mrs. Olmstead and the rest, not guilty. The judge thanked the

* Where the judge declares mistrial a second trial does not constitute double jeopardy because the accused has not yet had one full and complete trial.

jurors for their service and dismissed them. Turning to the convicted defendants, he announced that sentencing would be postponed for several weeks until he had had further opportunity to reflect on the case and to allow defense counsel to make any last-minute motions. When bail had been continued for those adjudged guilty, the court adjourned.

Interviewed by reporters after the trial, the foreman of the jury stated that "the telephone conversations virtually were disregarded."[6] Old Mr. York remarked wistfully as he left the courtroom, "It'll seem funny to go about without a bailiff." Roy Olmstead was probably experiencing the opposite reaction.

CHAPTER

5

Appeal

The Olmstead trial was over, but the Olmstead case was still very much alive. On March 5, 1926, two weeks after the verdict was returned, Olmstead, Finch, and six others filed a motion with Judge Neterer asking him to "arrest judgment"—to find that the verdict was erroneous because of a mistake in law—and to grant a new trial. The reasons counsel offered for these requests were essentially the same as those they had put forth in their pretrial maneuvers.

On March 8, Neterer denied each motion and imposed sentences. Olmstead received two years at hard labor on each of the two counts on which he had been convicted, the sentences to run consecutively, plus an $8000 fine and all the costs of prosecution on the second count of the indictment. Finch received three years, an $8000 fine, and costs. The other defendants were given jail terms ranging from eighteen months to three years, with fines of from $500 to $6000.

The defendants then appealed to the Circuit Court of Appeals for the Ninth Circuit, and Neterer, as is customary in non-capital offenses, allowed them to post bond guaranteeing appearance if the appeal failed; the defendants thus retained their freedom until the appellate court could decide their case. By law every loser in a federal district court has the right to one review of his case by a higher court, provided he can give a legal reason which is not trivial or obviously dilatory. In 1926 federal courts were organized in nine numbered judicial circuits, with an additional circuit in the District of Columbia. Within each circuit a Circuit Court of Appeals served as the appellate tribunal to review district court decisions. In 1926 these courts were staffed by three to seven judges, with three judges normally sitting to hear any particular case.* In rare instances involving extremely important issues of public law, all the judges of a circuit might sit together (*en banc* is the legal term) to hear the case. At the time of the *Olmstead* appeal, the Ninth Circuit included the state of Arizona, California, Idaho, Montana, Nevada, Oregon, and Washington.

On appeal in a criminal case, the convicted party cannot ask the reviewing court to reweigh the evidence and to second-guess the jury. He can ask the court to do one or both of two things: (1) to review the rulings and instructions of the trial judge and decide whether in construing the law he made errors of sufficient seriousness to justify granting a new trial or perhaps even the dismissal of the indictment; (2) to examine the evidence only to the extent of deciding whether or not twelve honest men could reasonably have arrived at a verdict of guilty. Generally speaking, an appellate court will take up only those questions specifically brought to its attention by the appellant,† and then only if the appellant

* At present the United States is divided into ten numbered circuits plus one for the District of Columbia. The Courts of Appeals (a 1947 statute dropped the word "Circuit" from the title) are staffed by three to nine judges.

† The appellant is the party who appeals; the appellee is the party who won in the trial court.

had raised those same questions at the trial.

In presenting his case to the Circuit Court of Appeals, each lawyer submits a written brief outlining and arguing the main points he wishes to make. Each side, if it cares to, may file a second set of briefs rebutting the assertions made by the other. When the briefs are in and the trial judge has forwarded a certified copy of the trial record, the clerk of the circuit court sets a date for oral argument. Counsel for both sides appear in court on the day appointed and elaborate on the points made in their written briefs. Because of the large number of cases they must hear, circuit judges limit the time of oral argument; usually, each side gets about an hour to present its case.

The defendants—now the appellants[1]—in the Olmstead case split into two different groups and appealed separately. Olmstead, Finch, and seven others brought one appeal; the remaining twelve brought a second action. The fundamental errors asserted by both groups, however, were pretty much the same: the pretrial motions should have been granted. Both groups repeated the earlier claims that the grand jury had considered improper and insufficient evidence and had been tampered with by a federal agent; the indictment had not accused the defendants of a criminal act; the trial judge should have ordered the full bill of particulars requested by the defendants; the search warrant should have been quashed; Finch and Olmstead should have had separate trials;* and the trial judge should not have allowed the government to introduce evidence obtained through wiretapping. Further, appellants listed certain errors at the trial, all of which revolved around the objections made to the use of the Black Book by the prosecution and prosecution witnesses. The second group of appel-

* Naturally, only Finch and Olmstead could make this particular point, since they were the only ones directly affected.

lants claimed additional procedural errors in that the testimony offered at the trial had mainly concerned only Olmstead and Finch and had not linked others to any conspiracy.

To hear the *Olmstead* appeal, William B. Gilbert, Senior Circuit Judge of the Ninth Circuit, appointed a three-judge panel composed of himself, Judge Frank H. Rudkin, and Judge Frank S. Dietrich. Gilbert, at seventy-nine was one of the oldest federal judges still on active service. Born in Fairfax County, Virginia, fourteen years before the outbreak of the Civil War, he had gone to Williams College in Massachusetts and then to law school at the University of Michigan. This latter education set him apart from many of his colleagues on the bench, since until near the end of the last century the typical way of preparing for a legal career was to "read" law in the office of a successful practitioner rather than to attend law school; Gilbert was, in fact, the only one of the three judges on this panel who had a law degree. After graduation from Michigan, he had moved to Portland, Oregon, where he practiced law and dabbled in politics; later he had been appointed by President Benjamin Harrison to the bench of the Ninth Circuit.

Frank H. Rudkin was seventeen years younger than Gilbert, but even so he had been born during the Civil War. A native of Vernon, Ohio, he had moved to Yakima, Washington, in 1887, just after he had finished "reading" law. In 1901 he became a judge on the county court, and four years later was elected to the state supreme court, serving as chief justice from 1909 to 1911. After his six-year term was over, Rudkin returned to private practice until President Coolidge appointed him a circuit judge in 1923.

Judge Dietrich was born in Kansas six months before the battle of Gettysburg. Law was to be a second career for him. After receiving his A.B. and A.M. from Brown

University, he returned to Kansas and for four years taught Latin, history, and political economy at Ottawa University. Soon, however, Dietrich began reading law, and after being admitted to the bar moved to Boise, Idaho, to practice. Theodore Roosevelt appointed him a federal district judge in 1907, and Coolidge promoted him to the circuit bench in 1926.

On May 9, 1927, after the briefs and reply briefs had been submitted and each side allowed oral argument, the Circuit Court of Appeals handed down its decisions in the two cases, now officially known as *Olmstead* v. *United States*[2] and *Green* v. *United States*.[3] By a vote of two to one the court affirmed all the convictions. Speaking for himself and Judge Dietrich, Gilbert filed an opinion that merely ticked off the points raised by the appellants as not well taken. Coming to the wiretapping issue, Gilbert stated that the prevailing rule was that evidence obtained by illegal means was not automatically inadmissible in court. Nor did the act of wiretapping itself constitute a violation of the Fourth Amendment's protection of privacy or the Fifth Amendment's protection against self-incrimination.

> The purpose of the amendments is to prevent the invasion of homes and offices and the seizure of incriminating evidence found therein. Whatever may be said of tapping of telephone wires as an unethical intrusion upon the privacy of persons who are suspected of crime, it is not an act which comes within the letter of the prohibition of constitutional provisions. It is not disputed that evidence obtained by the vision of one who sees through windows or open doors of a dwelling house is admissible. Nor has it been held that evidence obtained by listening at doors or windows is inadmissible. Evidence thus obtained is not believed to be

distinguishable from evidence obtained by listening in on telephone wires.[4]

In reply, Judge Rudkin wrote a respectful but sharply worded dissent. He began by noting that there was little doubt of the guilt of many of the defendants, but that this was not the issue before the court. The real issue was whether the defendants had received a fair trial free from serious legal error. And he found two major errors, one narrow, one broad. The trial judge had erred when he had allowed federal agents to use the Black Book while on the witness stand. Rudkin agreed that it was perfectly legitimate for a witness to refresh his memory, but by the government's own admission entries in this volume had been re-arranged. Since the witnesses who used the book had not taken part in the editing process, they had no knowledge whether the meaning of their contemporary notes had been distorted. Moreover, Rudkin thought that the trial record showed that the witnesses had little if any independent recollection of events about which they were testifying. It was apparent, the judge said, "that the book and not the witnesses was speaking. A better opportunity to color or fabricate testimony could not well be devised by the wit of man."

It was on the broader issue, however, that Rudkin placed the main burden of his dissent. In general he agreed with the majority that how a witness obtained evidence was of no concern to a court, but the Supreme Court had established certain exceptions. The most important, and most relevant, was the *Weeks* rule, so named because it had been laid down in the case of *Weeks* v. *United States* in 1914.[5] This rule provided that evidence obtained in violation of constitutional commands could not be used in a *federal* court. Only by excluding this sort of evidence, the justices had reasoned, could the guarantees of the Fourth and Fifth

Amendments be made effective. Knowledge that the evidence could not be used in court against a suspect would prevent federal officials from acting unconstitutionally, while the prospects of prosecution for such activity were too small to be an effective deterrent.

The Supreme Court had announced this rule not as a matter of constitutional law, but as a principle to govern the administration of justice in federal courts. Thus the *Weeks* rule did not forbid state courts to consider unconstitutionally obtained evidence. But, Rudkin continued, since the Olmstead case had been tried in a federal court the *Weeks* rule had to be applied because wiretapping abridged rights protected by the Fourth and Fifth Amendments. The majority had contended that since the wiretapping activities of the prohibition agents had not caused them to trespass on Olmstead's property or to take any of his physical possessions, there had been no violation of his rights under the Fourth or Fifth Amendment. In rebuttal Rudkin pointed out that the chief purpose of these amendments "was not the protection of property, but the protection of the individual in his liberty and in the privacies of life." Closing his opinion, the judge waxed eloquent:

> A person using the telegraph or telephone is not broadcasting to the world. His conversation is sealed from the public as completely as the nature of the instrumentalities employed will permit, and no federal officer or federal agent has a right to take his message from the wires, in order that it may be used against him. Such a situation would be deplorable and intolerable, to say the least. . . . If ills such as these must be borne, our forefathers signally failed in their desire to ordain and establish a government to secure the blessings of liberty to themselves and their posterity.[6]

Rudkin's dissent probably stirred the hearts of civil libertarians. But his had been only one vote out of three, and on appellate courts, unlike juries, unanimity is not required. The majority, however narrow, decides the case, and two of the three judges on the Circuit Court of Appeals had decided that Olmstead and his associates had been lawfully tried and convicted. Since the ferocity and futility of the federal government's war against liquor traffic made it foolish even to consider trying to secure a presidential pardon, there was only one more hope for the defendants: review by the United States Supreme Court.

Before 1925 it had been relatively easy for a litigant with money and patience to get his case before the Supreme Court by hiring a skillful lawyer and following his advice, since the justices had little to say about whether or not they would take a case. If a lawyer could meet standard jurisdictional criteria, the justices had to grant him a hearing, no matter how trivial the issue and how busy they themselves were with problems of national concern. Because of this system, which made an appeal a matter of right in so many instances, the Court was more than a year behind in its docket when William Howard Taft became Chief Justice in 1921. Future prospects were that, as appeals from prohibition prosecutions increased, the justices would fall even further behind.

The new Chief Justice immediately began talking to some of his old friends in Congress about the necessity for a drastic overhaul of the Court's jurisdiction; at the same time he appointed a committee of the justices to draw up the needed legislation. When the committee's work was done, Taft sent the bill to his friends and had it introduced in Congress. He then proceeded to conduct a vigorous and astute lobbying campaign. Not only did he and other justices testify before congressional committees about the proposal; the Chief Justice also took his case to the country and made a series of public speeches urging support of what had become known as the Judges' Bill. In addition, Taft worked closely with the chief lobbyist for the American Bar Association as well as with the Attorney General and the Solicitor General of the United States. The Chief Justice kept the legislative pot boiling by writing literally dozens of letters to senators, congressmen, and newspapermen.

When legislators appeared uninterested in the Court's proposal, Taft took to patrolling the halls of Congress, buttonholing influential solons and cajoling them into supporting his measure. (This task was made easier by the fact that until 1935 the Court was located in the Senate wing of the Capitol Building, one floor below the present Senate chamber.) Through his old friend Attorney General Harry Daugherty, Taft even persuaded Coolidge to allow him to draft a few paragraphs strongly supporting adoption of the Judges' Bill for the President's annual message to Congress. The Chief Justice's persistence finally paid off when the House passed the measure in late 1924. When it came up for a vote in the Senate, Taft was still furiously lobbying and, by making concessions to the opposition, was able to secure passage in early February 1925 by the lopsided vote of 76 to 1.

After the 1925 act, cases could reach the Supreme Court in one of three ways—certification, appeal, or certiorari. A Circuit Court of Appeals may send—or certify—to the Supreme Court a question of law presented in a case before it, if that question is of such import that the Circuit judges feel it demands an immediate answer by the highest court in the country. Circuit judges have seldom certified questions to the Court under this procedure; when they have, the justices have sometimes refused to pass on the issue, expressing a desire to have the benefit of the Circuit judges' wisdom before attempting to answer such difficult problems.

In an appeal, a losing litigant carries his case to the Supreme Court and, as a matter of right, demands that the Court hear his plea. The great reform of the 1925 act was in limiting the kinds of cases the justices had to take to three principal categories: (1) where a federal court has declared that a state statute, order, or constitutional provision violates the federal Constitution; (2) where a state court has invalidated all or part of a federal statute, order, or treaty; (3) where a state court has sustained the constitutionality of a state statute, order, or constitutional provision against a "substantial" challenge that it violates the federal Constitution. In practice, the Court finds a large number of challenges under this third category to be insubstantial and very frequently refuses to take such cases. Indeed, much to the annoyance of many lawyers, the Court generally treats an appeal less as a matter of right, as the statute reads, than as a privilege to be granted or denied as the justices see fit.

Almost all cases presenting a question of federal statutory or constitutional law must thus come to the Court through the third avenue, a petition for a writ of certiorari. The decision to grant or deny the petition—and so to agree or refuse to hear the case—is completely within the discretion of the Court, and the justices rarely give reasons for their refusals to grant the writ. According to the Court's rules, petitions will be granted only where the case presents a question which is significant for general public policy in the United States, not merely because the issue is of importance to the individual litigants. The result of this procedure is to give the justices almost complete control over their docket.

The rules of the Court in effect during the 1927 term

provided that a losing litigant in a Circuit Court of Appeals could petition for certiorari within ninety days of the decision in the lower court. The petition itself, the justices stipulated, "shall contain only a summary and short statement of the matter involved and the reasons relied on for the allowance of the writ." An indexed copy of the trial record was also required, and either party, if he so desired, might file a supporting brief, provided it was "direct, concise," and printed in large type with wide margins to ease the work of the weary eyes of the justices.[7]

The Supreme Court meets from the first Monday in October and stays in session until all the cases on its docket are disposed of or until the justices are completely exhausted. In the 1920s, Taft was usually able to adjourn the Court by the end of May; today, the press of business may keep the justices in Washington until the middle of July. During a term, the Court is normally in session for two weeks to hear oral argument, then recesses for about two weeks so that the justices can research, think, and write opinions.

In the 1920s, the justices heard argument Mondays through Fridays from noon until 4:30, with a half hour break for lunch. On Saturdays they would meet in conference to discuss and vote on the cases they had heard argued during the previous week. More recently, the justices meet at 10 A.M. and hear cases until 2:30 P.M., Monday through Thursday. Fridays and sometimes Saturdays are taken up by conference discussions. Then Monday was the day on which decisions were announced. The present practice is for decisions to be announced whenever the formal opinions are ready. In the 1920s the justices commonly read their opinions almost in full, though this practice has gradually given way to a short summary or a bare statement of result.

After the decisions are announced, the Court proceeds to hear oral argument.

It is at the conferences at the end of the week that petitions for certiorari are voted on. Since the Court gets a very large number of such petitions (the number is now about 2000 a term) the justices quickly found that they could not devote much time to discussing any single one. Charles Evans Hughes, Taft's successor as Chief Justice, developed the current practice of circulating a "special list" before each conference. This list contains cases the Chief Justice feels are too trivial to be worth discussing; if no justice informs the Chief of his disagreement, these petitions are denied without further action. An objection from any justice is sufficient to strike a case from the special list and bring it up for consideration at the conference.

When a petition is considered at conference, the Chief Justice usually says a few sentences summarizing the case and giving his views. Unless the case is of extreme importance there will be little debate, and the Chief quickly calls for a vote. Four votes, one less than a majority, are sufficient to grant the writ, and sometimes if even one or two justices are strongly in favor of granting the petition, the majority will acquiesce.

The closeness of the division in the Circuit Court of Appeals and the power of Rudkin's dissent encouraged the defendants to try to get their case before the Supreme Court. By now Olmstead and his associates had divided into three groups. All three pressed the argument that wiretapping was unconstitutional and such evidence should not have been admitted at the trial, but each had other specific objections to the trial procedure. Each of the groups filed a petition for certiorari. The petition of Olmstead, Finch, and their associates made five basic points:

(a) That this [constitutionality of wiretapping] is a question not only of grave constitutional law, but one of supreme importance to the general public;
(b) That this question has never been passed upon by any Court, except as it was passed upon by the said District Court and the Circuit Court of Appeals for the Ninth Circuit, in the instant case, and it was only decided by a majority of 2–1 . . . ;
(c) That it is a Federal question, and has been decided in a way in conflict with applicable decisions of this Court;
(d) That the decision of the said Circuit Court of Appeals is untenable;
(e) That the question is an important one of Federal law which has not been, but should be, decided by the Supreme Court of the nation.[8]

In their supporting briefs the defendants—now called "petitioners" since they were petitioning for certiorari—relied heavily on the language of Judge Rudkin's dissent, stressing the fact that wiretapping was a crime in the state of Washington, and arguing further that Judge Neterer should not have allowed prosecution witnesses to use the Black Book at the trial. These initial efforts were fruitless. On Monday, November 21, 1927, among the memoranda orders issued by the Supreme Court was one which read simply:

Roy Olmstead, Jerry L. Finch, Clarence G. Healy et al., Petitioners, v. United States of America [#493]; Charles S. Green, Emory A. Kern, Z. J. Hendrick et al., Petitioners, v. United States of America [#532]; and Edward H. McInnis, Petitioner, v. United States of America [#533]

> Petitions for Writs of Certiorari to the United States Circuit Court of Appeals for the Ninth Circuit. . . . Denied.[9]

The bad news hit Olmstead just when he had thought that the world was once again opening up for him. He had failed to appear for a second trial on a set of charges growing out of the same general evidence which had led to his conviction on the conspiracy counts. When later apprehended he had been forced to stand trial on these new charges, but on November 17, just four days before the Supreme Court had denied certiorari, the jury in the second case had acquitted him.

Almost as soon as the Supreme Court's refusal to take the case was announced, federal agents arrested Olmstead and he had to spend the night in jail. Thomas Revelle claimed that Olmstead was about to flee the country and asked the district judge to hold the prisoner without bond, pending actual receipt of the Supreme Court's order (usually it takes from six to seven weeks for the formal papers to be prepared). At this point Olmstead decided to give up the fight and to start serving his sentence. He was taken to the federal penitentiary at McNeil Island, Washington.

Some of Olmstead's former colleagues, however, were still not willing to quit. Supreme Court rules then in effect provided that, within forty days of a decision,* the losing party could apply for a rehearing, and two of the three groups of petitioners availed themselves of this opportunity. They argued:

> That the constitutional question involved in this case has such a far-reaching effect upon the economic and social life of the nation that it should be unqualifiedly determined by the decisions of this Honorable Court. It affects the home and business

* Now the Court allows only twenty-five days.

> life of every member of this Court and every man and woman living in the United States. If the action of Government agents in tapping private telephone lines is stamped by the Court as lawful, then the personal, private and confidential communications of the millions of people who use the telephone daily will be subject to the scrutiny of Government agents acting under the guise of attempting to obtain information related to crime. It requires no stretch of the imagination to visualize the statement of Circuit Judge Rudkin that "such a situation would be deplorable and intolerable, to say the least."

Because of the care with which each justice examines a case before voting on it, petitions for rehearing are rarely granted; and it came as no surprise when on January 3, 1928, the Court denied the rehearing request from the first group of petitioners. On January 9, however, government officials were shocked when the justices issued a new order:

> This Court now reconsiders all these three petitions for certiorari and grants the writs therein, limiting their consideration, however, to the question whether the use of evidence of private telephone conversations between the defendants and others, intercepted by means of wire tapping, is a violation of the 4th and 5th Amendments, and, therefore, not permissible in the Federal courts.[10]

Thus the case had been narrowed to one issue—the constitutionality of wiretapping, and it was on this single point that counsel for both sides were ordered to focus their arguments. On the day after the Supreme Court's decision to hear the case, the *Seattle Daily Times* published a long editorial:

> The real issue in the matter . . . is the privacy of telephonic communication in general. If wires may be tapped for one reason or on the strength of any one's suspicion, they may be tapped for all reasons and suspicions and for none. . . . Every law-abiding and decent telephone patron is concerned in this matter. If they are to be subject to eavesdropping annoyance, they will at least wish to know it so that they may govern themselves accordingly.

Meanwhile, Roy Olmstead was released from McNeil Island on bond, once more—temporarily—a free man.

CHAPTER

6

The Taft Court

It is customary in the literature on the American judiciary to refer to the Supreme Court during a specific time period by the name of the Chief Justice. Thus we often read about the Marshall Court, the Hughes Court, the Vinson Court, and the Warren Court. To a greater extent than is true in most instances, the Court during the 1920s deserved the title of the Taft Court. As President, Taft had appointed several of the associate justices with whom he was to sit, though by the time the Olmstead case was decided only Willis Van Devanter was still on the bench. As Chief Justice, Taft had played an important part in selecting three of the other justices who would hear and vote on Roy Olmstead's legal arguments.

Taft had also been more than a passive candidate for the Court himself. He had been helped by fate, but he had also done his very best to help fate help him. The center chair on the Court had been his lifelong ambition; he had always desired it far more even than the White House. In 1910, when he nominated his old friend Edward Douglass White for the Chief Justiceship, Taft could not keep from commenting on the bitter irony of his bestowing upon another the one public office he himself coveted. White, perhaps moved by the magnanimity of a Unitarian Ohio Republican's appointing a Catholic Democrat from Louisiana, promised the President that he would resign when another Republican was in the White House, so that Taft might have an opportunity to attain his life's ambition.

Shortly after the Republican victory in the 1920 campaign, President-Elect Warren G. Harding had told Taft that he could have the Chief Justiceship. There was only one small hitch: White, despite some tactful hints from his former benefactor, apparently could not recall any agreement to step down.

Time, however, would soon accomplish what memory and gratitude could not. By the late spring of 1921, White, seventy-six years old, infirm, nearly deaf and going blind, died in office. But once again Taft's plans were temporarily frustrated. It seemed that Harding, in his anxiousness to please everyone, had made a double promise. He had pledged Taft the Chief Justiceship and had earlier promised George Sutherland, one of his campaign managers in the 1920 race, the first vacancy on the Court. Harding's dilemma was heightened by his knowledge that both men desperately wanted the center chair. Taft's ambition had been common knowledge in Washington (and Ohio) for over twenty years; to complicate matters, so Harding told a confidant, Sutherland was "crazy" to be Chief Justice.[1] Since he had specifically promised the Chief Justiceship to Taft, Harding realized that Sutherland would have to step aside. Nevertheless, the President tried a series of maneuvers to lessen the hurt to his former adviser. According to one Washington rumor, the President was considering appointing old Justice Rufus Day as Chief Justice and naming Sutherland to fill Day's chair. Day, so the story went, would resign after a year, and Harding could then appoint Taft Chief Justice. Taft wanted no part of any such plan. Recalling White's lapse of memory, Taft, who was almost sixty-four and already beyond the age which he himself, when President, had claimed was too old for a new appointee to the bench, commented: "That is trifling with a great office, and I don't favor any such arrangement."[2]

Whether or not the Day rumor was true, the President was trying to arrange for a resignation of one of the associate justices, either Joseph McKenna or Oliver Wendell Holmes, so that Sutherland and Taft might be nominated simultaneously. These efforts were frustrated, and as the weeks dragged on Taft began to despair. His despondency deepened when he heard reports that Charles Evans Hughes was a candidate and that the White House was seething with intrigue over the vacancy. In this kind of in-fighting, Taft should have had no fear of giving as good as he took, for with his active cooperation a number of his friends, including Gus Karger, his old White House press secretary, Thomas Shelton, chief lobbyist for the American Bar Association, Senator Frank Brandegee of the Senate Judiciary Committee, and Attorney General Harry Daugherty, were all pressing Harding to appoint Taft and to do so quickly. The President finally gave in, and on June 30, 1921 sent Taft's name to the Senate. Confirmation came without a serious struggle; only four senators voting against the ex-President.

Needless to say, Taft was ecstatic, but not so enthralled by his good fortune as to neglect the opportunity to make a gracious overture to Sutherland. The disappointed candidate had wired his congratulations, and Taft immediately sent a handwritten reply: "I look forward to having you on the bench with me. I know as you do that the President intends to put you there. . . . Our views are much alike and it is important that they prevail."[3]

Some of the other justices were less than euphoric over Taft's good fortune. Justice Louis D. Brandeis must have pondered the situation with deep misgivings. As a young progressive lawyer, he had acutely embarrassed the Taft administration by exposing its botching of conservation policies in the Ballinger–Pinchot controversy—an exposure that deepened the developing break between Taft and Theodore Roosevelt and eventually led to Taft's defeat for reelection in 1912. A few years later Taft had been one of a group of former presidents of the American Bar Association who publicly had urged the Senate to reject Wilson's nomination of Brandeis to the Supreme Court, claiming he lacked "judicial temperament." Again in 1920, when campaigning for Harding, Taft had attacked Brandeis, this time for favoring "socialistic raids" on private property rights. Sitting on the bench and attending conferences presided over by his ancient antagonist may have posed a challenge to Brandeis' good nature and intellectual powers, but the signs did not augur for a harmonious relationship.

Justice Holmes had less personally oriented doubts. He had heard that Taft was lazy and that he was difficult to get along with if one disagreed with him. Most important, the old justice questioned the new Chief's intellectual capacity. "I never saw anything," Holmes remarked about Taft to a friend, "that struck me as more than first rate second rate."[4] After the first meeting of the Court, however, Holmes modified his pessimism, concluding that "the new C. J. promises well. Perhaps the main question as to a C. J. is his way of disposing of executive details, and Taft seems likely to take them easily and get through them without friction."[5] By the end of Taft's first term, Holmes confessed that the work had never gone so smoothly in his eighteen years on the Court, and he delighted the Chief Justice by telling him so. Brandeis, too, was more than willing to appear, at least, to forget the past. Within a week of the opening of the Court, Taft wrote his brother, "Brandeis and I are on excellent terms . . . honors are easy."[6]

The favorable impression Taft made as an administrator was no accident. While nurturing his ambition over the years, Taft had also been developing a concept of the office of Chief Justice. Probably no man came to the bench more sure of the policy objectives he wanted to accomplish and more certain of how best to accomplish them. The Chief Justiceship, he thought, was the most important position in American government. "I am the head of the judicial branch of government," he said in 1921, and from the beginning he acted in a manner befitting that station. Holmes's fear that Taft was indolent could not have been more wrong. The Chief Justice's huge bulk and placid smile camouflaged a vast store of disciplined energy. He plunged into the work of the Court and in an effort to clean up the crowded docket took on himself far more than his fair share of opinions to write.

Deciding individual cases, Taft knew, was not a final remedy for the situation in which the federal courts found themselves. The Supreme Court, like most federal tribunals, was far behind in its docket; and since he saw that if courts were to be the main instruments of American government—and he firmly believed that they should be—then the instruments would have to be freshly honed to fulfill their proper function. Working with other judges and Justice Department officials, the Chief Justice helped draft a series of proposals for new legislation. First was a three-pronged bill to increase the number of district judges, to give the Chief Justice greater authority to assign judges to temporary duty in districts where dockets were jammed, and to provide for an annual conference of senior circuit judges with the Chief Justice to supply an "executive principle" and iron out difficulties in judicial administration. Next, Taft appointed a committee of justices to draft a new statute completely revising the appellate jurisdiction of the Supreme Court and establishing the certiorari system described in the previous chapter. Third, the Chief helped draw up a bill by which Congress would delegate to the justices primary authority to establish rules of procedure for all lower federal courts. Finally, he made a series of proposals to raise the pay of federal judges and to take care of some minor items of administration.

Not content with participating in the genesis of these plans, Taft had lobbied as incessantly for each of them as he had for the Judges' Bill. These tactics enabled him to persuade Congress to adopt the first two of his bills in the Judiciary Acts of 1922 and 1925 and to obtain a substantial pay raise for judges. The third piece of legislation, the procedural bill, was not enacted until four years after his death. The Chief Justice used similar lobbying techniques to defeat several proposals he felt would endanger the judicial system.

Impersonal reform of the judicial system was not enough for a man with Taft's extroverted personality. "Teamwork" was his goal, his constant slogan for the judiciary. Soon after becoming Chief Justice he began to establish a high degree of rapport with lower court judges—a group, he knew, who could check the power of the Supreme Court in much the same fashion as the executive bureaucracy can hamstring a President. By the end of 1921 he had sent a cordial personal letter to every federal district judge, asking for suggestions on needed reforms in court procedure. He also wrote to every senior circuit judge requesting advice and information on problems pertaining to overcrowded dockets. "I am very anxious," Taft told his fellow judges, "to introduce teamwork among the Federal Judges of the country, and I call upon you to help me in this matter."[7] He carefully and promptly acknowledged every reply and sometimes discussed individual suggestions.

Taft was also solicitous of the state bench. He wrote the chief justice of each state, noting that he had instructed the clerk to send to every state supreme court the opinions of the U.S. Supreme Court. In return, he requested that the reports of state decisions be forwarded to Washington. "I feel," Taft explained, "as if the Judges in the Courts of last resort in this country should be brought more closely together, and that [an exchange of opinions] would facilitate a mutual understanding."[8]

The Chief was equally concerned about relations with the executive department. He quickly got on a "Dear Harry" basis with Attorney General Daugherty and obtained a pledge—not always honored—to be consulted whenever a federal judicial appointment was under consideration. (Despite his own political experience and the closeness of his contacts with the Attorney General, Taft apparently had no real idea about the extent of corruption in the Department of Justice, and he was genuinely shocked when, some years later, he learned the full story of the Harding-Daugherty regime.)

The Chief Justice was also a frequent visitor at the White House, advising first Harding, then Coolidge, about affairs of state ranging from American participation in the World Court, to a new ambassador for Germany, to a new Solicitor General, to a pardon for a man whose conviction the justices had felt legally unable to reverse, to vetoes of veterans' bonus legislation, the Mc-

Nary–Haugen Bill, and tax reform measures—all this in addition to judicial appointments. As the Chief told his son, "I can not keep my mind out of politics, especially when I have no responsibility about it."[9]

Taft's policy objectives were simple and clear cut. Twenty years earlier he had been politically left of center. He had moved somewhat to the right in the intervening decades, but the world had moved even farther to the left, leaving him well to the right of center politically, though he was usually a staunch supporter of the national government when questions arose over federal versus state authority. In the 1920s Taft believed even more strongly than he had when in the White House that the principal function of the Supreme Court was to "preserve the fundamental structure of our government as our fathers gave it to us."[10] To accomplish this aim, the court system had to be able to act efficiently—which in large part explains the Chief Justice's perennial interest in judicial reform.[11] And acting efficiently meant that judges be alert to protect property rights against government interference, particularly interference from state government. Because he was an advocate of national authority, Taft would tolerate a broader range of congressional regulation of interstate commerce than would most of his conservative colleagues, but his views on the proper sphere of government regulation of local business operations were exceedingly narrow. "The cornerstone of our Civilization," he told Elihu Root, "is the proper maintenance of the guarantees of the 14th Amendment and the 5th Amendment."[12]

Influencing lower court judges, executive officials, and members of Congress would be to little avail, Taft knew, if he were in a minority of the Court on issues he considered important. Generally speaking, however, a majority of the other justices shared his conservative political ideology, and when vacancies occurred on the High Bench he took special care to make certain that Harding and Coolidge would select conservatives.

Despite this over-all advantage, Taft still faced two problems in dealing with the other justices. First, merely being in the majority was not enough for him. Two drives coalesced here, one psychological, the other political. Taft was shrewd and, if need be, tough, but he was also a charming man who tried to understand, if not love, each of his fellow men and expected and needed similar efforts in return. Like every intelligent man he did not expect that all people would always agree with him. Nevertheless, he abhorred unpleasantness or public airing of disputes. He took pride in his real ability to reach amicable compromises with those with whom he disagreed. Few men ever saw Taft lose his temper. During the week he exuded patience, tact, and camaraderie. On Sunday mornings he would write long letters to his brothers and children and release his tensions in a series of rancorous explosions about the ill will and shortsightedness of those with whom a cruel fate had forced him to cooperate.

The political factor was as important as the psychological. Taft knew that much of the Court's power rested on the myth that the justices merely "found" the law—that, as John Marshall had claimed,[13] the justices exercised judgment, not will. If the justices split into angry factions, hurling charges of error and judicial legislation at one another, this myth would be shaken, if not shattered, and the Court's power correspondingly reduced.

Thus unanimity of decision was a doubly vital consideration for Taft. When he was in the minority he would usually stifle his views and acquiesce, and he wanted his colleagues to do the same. When in the majority, he would go to great lengths to negotiate with potential dissenters, to win them over by editing his opinions and making concessions. His goal was again teamwork—nine oarsmen, each pulling his own weight in the boat.

A second and closely related problem was that of leading the justices to the "correct" decision in specific and very complex cases in which conservatives might sharply differ among themselves. The Chief Justice, Taft wrote shortly before his own appointment, "is the head of the Court, and while his vote counts but one in the nine, he is, if he be a man of strong and persuasive personality, abiding convictions, recognized by learning and statesmanlike foresight, expected to promote teamwork by the Court, so as to give weight and solidarity to its opinions."[14]

Giving weight, solidarity, and direction to the work of the Court was no easy task, for, as Holmes had surmised, Taft, in spite of his native shrewdness, great energy, personal charm, and clarity of purpose, was neither an intellectual giant nor a gifted legal craftsman. As a young man he had served for three years as a state judge and later for eight years as a federal circuit judge. Although during that time he had been a very competent lawyer and judge, he had been away from the more technical aspects of law for over twenty years; now he had neither the time nor the disposition so to immerse himself in esoteric legal literature as to become an expert technician. His forte—and he knew it—was persuading those who disagreed to act like reasonable men of good will and strive for consensus. He simply could not successfully match his erudition against that of most of his colleagues, and when he tried to do so, he confessed to his son, the other justices would "humiliate" him.

Perhaps consciously, perhaps unconsciously, Taft arrived at part of a solution to his problem through a close alliance with Justice Willis Van Devanter, whom he had appointed to the Court in 1910. Although they were approximately the same age and both were graduates of the Cincinnati Law School and had been lower court judges, the two were in most ways very different. Taft had spent much of his life in the arena of partisan politics. Van Devanter, too, had been active in Republican party politics in Wyoming, but since going to the federal circuit bench in 1903, he had, formally at least, stayed out of party politics. As adamant a conservative as Taft, Van Devanter was also a lawyer's lawyer, able to rattle precedents off the tip of his tongue and to distinguish them according to fine, hair-splitting logic. Without consulting references, he could lay out in detail relevant jurisdictional statutes and fill in the gaps with succinct accounts of actual practice on the point. Taft was continually dazzled by the scope of Van Devanter's encyclopedic mind, and the Chief Justice quickly learned how to exploit this store of knowledge. Soon Taft would be affectionately referring to Van Devanter as "my chancellor," and, in the bosom of his family, would express doubts that the Court might not be run more efficiently were Van Devanter in the center chair.

But if Taft needed Van Devanter's erudition, Van Devanter needed Taft's talents to complete his own personality and maximize his influence on public policy. For all his immense learning, Van Devanter suffered from pen paralysis. At conference he was brilliant. Alone in his study and faced with the agonies of literary creation, his mind became as blank as the paper at which he stared. As an editor, however, his brilliance once again shone, and his pen could race with his thoughts. Thus the two men formed a most fruitful partnership. Taft would give his laboriously written first drafts to his "dear friend," and Van Devanter would remove most of the infelicitous phrases that came so easily to the Chief Justice, add suggestions for finer legal reasoning, and supply the needed authorities to buttress the conclusions at which Taft instinctively arrived.

At the opposite end of the Court's ideological spectrum was another pair of friends, Holmes and Brandeis. They tended to vote together on socioeconomic issues, but their votes were products of very different reasoning processes. Holmes was a detached, skeptical, at times even cynical, philosopher. A confirmed relativist, he refused to write his own economic theories into constitutional law. "The fourteenth amendment does not enact Mr. Herbert Spencer's *Social Statics*," was his vain protest against the Court's reading *laissez faire* and Social Darwinism into the Constitution in *Lochner* v. *New York* (1905).[15] Although he believed that most governmental efforts to regulate business were futile at best and silly at worst—in private, for instance, he referred to the Sherman Act as "humbug"—he still voted to uphold the constitutionality of statutes which could have been enacted by reasonable men. For him, government regulation of business should be judged by whether Congress or state legislatures had authority to enact such laws, not by whether such legislation was likely to be wise or stupid, effective or ineffective. "His judicial philosophy of leaving the legislature alone," Max Lerner has written, "came from a deeper philosophy of leaving the cosmos alone."[16]

What Holmes tolerated—social and economic experimentation—Brandeis fervently believed in. He had made his reputation as a lawyer who fought for liberal causes. Perhaps the statement that best capsules Brandeis' approach to economic issues was his vain remonstrance against his brethren's attachment to *laissez faire:* "If we would guide by the light of reason, we must let our minds be bold."[17] Where social or economic legislation was involved, Brandeis remained as much of an advocate for governmental freedom to experiment as his more conservative colleagues were advocates of preserving the status quo. "I told him long ago," Holmes once commented about his friend, "that he was really an advocate rather than a judge. He is affected by his interest in a cause, and if he feels it he is not detached." But detached or involved, Holmes added, Brandeis' "interests are noble, and as you say, his insights profound."[18]

Holmes and Brandeis differed in other respects. In their approach to cases Holmes was essentially a philosopher, Brandeis an empiricist. By his own admission, Holmes hated facts. Brandeis revelled in them; statistics and ledger books were as much his joy as they were Holmes's despair. As a lawyer Brandeis had used these tools to such an advantage that a legal argument based mainly on economic or sociological evidence is still known as a Brandeis brief. As a judge he was constantly adding to his store of knowledge about societal organization and operations. During vacations while Holmes would relax and read Proust or Rousseau, Brandeis would pore over the latest report of the U.S. Coal Commission.

Despite their differences, or perhaps because of them, Holmes and Brandeis were kindred spirits. Knowing their reputations as liberal judges, Taft had not looked forward to working with them. Yet to his surprise, the Chief immediately found relations with Brandeis outwardly pleasant and soon began to develop a genuine and lasting affection for Holmes. Each of them, Taft noted, "pulls his weight" on the Court, something some of the more conservative justices did not always do. Indeed, next to Taft himself, Holmes and Brandeis wrote the most opinions for the Court during the 1921–1929 terms.

Of the two, Holmes was the more eloquent and the more rapid writer. Working standing up at a special desk, the old gentleman—he was eighty when Taft came to the Court—would compose an opinion in a matter of hours. He would fret if an opinion assigned to him on Saturday had not been written, revised, printed, read and edited by his eight associates, and ready for approval at conference the following Saturday.

As the years went on, Taft's affection for Holmes deepened, but his personal opinion of Brandeis reverted to suspicion and distrust. In part this change was due to Brandeis' apparent influence with Holmes and, later, with young Justice Harlan Fiske Stone. "I am very fond of the old gentleman," Taft remarked about Holmes in 1928, "but he is so completely under the control of Brother Brandeis that it gives Brandeis two votes instead of one."[19] (But even though Holmes admitted that on economic issues Brandeis was apt to "bully" him a bit,[20] Taft was simply wrong in thinking that anyone could dominate the old Yankee.) In part the Chief Justice's distaste for Brandeis also grew out of the latter's persistence in asserting his constitutional views against those of the majority, and his skeptical attitude toward Taft's efforts at judicial reform. "Brandeis tries to be a good fellow," the Chief remarked caustically when his colleague expressed doubts about the certiorari bill, "but he misses every now and then."[21]

Although Brandeis' opinions were sufficiently annoying to Taft that he occasionally, in private, made an antisemitic remark about his associate, their outward relations went along smoothly during the entire period they served together. It was with James C. McReynolds that Taft had the greatest personal difficulties, though McReynolds was overtly rude to other justices rather than to Taft himself. Born in Kentucky during the Civil War and educated at the University of Virginia, McReynolds had been Woodrow Wilson's Attorney General. In that post he had earned a liberal reputation for his vigorous enforcement of the Sherman Anti-Trust Act.

Two explanations have been offered for Wilson's appointing McReynolds to the Court. The first was that the President wanted a justice with strong antimonopoly views. If this explanation is true, McReynolds lived up to his liberal promise, though only and absolutely only in the antitrust field. Antimonopoly prosecutions were almost the sole governmental regulations of business he would countenance. Indeed, McReynolds was so *laissez faire* that even Taft thought him a reactionary. McReynolds' approach to economic cases was best explained in a dissent in 1934 in which he frankly stated that the Court must consider the wisdom of a statute.[22] And he was likely to view any policy but Social Darwinism as patently unwise, if not downright foolish.

The second explanation for Wilson's appointing McReynolds to the bench was that he was too powerful to fire but too obnoxious to work with. There is some evidence to support this hypothesis. Holmes claimed that McReynolds was a kindly man, and he did contribute heavily to private and public charities, but most people found him a churlish boor. Taft described him as "selfish to the last degree, an able man, but fuller of prejudice than any man I have ever known, and one who seems to delight in making others uncomfortable. He has no high sense of duty. He is a continual grouch, and . . . really seems to have less of a loyal spirit to the Court than anybody."[23] Perhaps most annoying to Taft and frustrating of his desire to keep the Court functioning at the most efficient pace possible was McReynolds' refusal to place the Court above his personal pleasure. As a bachelor unused to regulating his life to accommodate others, he would, for instance, take off and go hunting on Chesapeake Bay when the ducks were calling, leaving the Chief Justice to fume over opinions unread and unwritten.

Bitterly antisemitic, McReynolds feuded constantly with Brandeis, with whom, of course, he was very likely to disagree strongly on constitutional issues. By the early 1920s, however, perhaps in part due to Taft's good-natured influence, McReynolds and Brandeis had reached a modus vivendi. They stopped arguing in conference and carried on their feud in eloquent silence. Despite McReynolds' selfishness and bigotry, he was an able craftsman and a worthy intellectual opponent, though one less likely to express his opinions in tightly reasoned syllogisms than in curt sarcasm.

The remaining four justices, George Sutherland, Pierce Butler, Edward Terry Sanford, and Harlan Fiske Stone, had come to the Court after Taft, and the Chief Justice had had a hand in the choice of each of them, though only indirectly for Sutherland in the sense that he kept him out of the center chair. Sutherland was a former senator from Utah and had been one of Harding's principal strategists in the 1920 campaign. Born in England in 1862, Sutherland was the first foreign-born justice in almost a hundred years. A one-time president of the American Bar Association, he was a craftsman in his own right, with a skill that compared favorably to Van Devanter's. Unlike Van Devanter, however, Sutherland's knowledge was coupled with an ability to write freely in a brisk, lucid style.

Like Taft, Sutherland was directed toward a definite policy goal—the carving out of the maximum amount of individual (that is, business) freedom from government regulations; and to Sutherland the "maximum" was very large indeed. His biographer aptly subtitled Sutherland's life story "A Man against the State."[24] He would approve government intervention against strikes or other labor activities, and he would go along with government assistance to business in the form of protective tariffs; but statutes like minimum wage requirements for women which restricted business freedom were anathema to him. Freedom of contract, he said in striking down a minimum wage law, is "the general rule and restraint the exception; and the exercise of legislative authority to bridge it can be justified only by the existence of exceptional circumstances."[25]

Because of Sutherland's economic philosophy and his readiness as a judge to read it into the Constitution, and because as a senator he had voted against Brandeis' nomination to the Court, one might have expected another McReynolds–Brandeis situation; but almost the reverse was true. Sutherland was a gentleman and was soon on pleasant terms with Brandeis and developed an even more amiable relationship with Holmes. As Justice Stone—with whom Sutherland had disagreed as consistently as with Brandeis and Holmes—told his sons when Sutherland decided to retire: "I shall see him go with regret. He is a man of fine character, genial temper; he did the work of the Court with a great thoroughness and fidelity, and he always made important contributions to the work of the Court."[26]

Pierce Butler was an Irish Catholic. Born in a log cabin in Dakota County, Minnesota in 1866, he was the only member of the Taft Court to come from a humble economic background.[27] After working his way through Carleton College, he had "read" law, and after a short career in politics settled down to become a prosperous railroad attorney. Van Devanter had known Butler when he was a circuit judge, and Taft had met him in an arbitration case. When a vacancy occurred on the Court in 1922, Taft began his own screening of candidates. Following his penchant for crossing party lines—"Uncle Joe" Cannon, the tyrannical Speaker of the House, had once commented that if Taft had been Pope he would have appointed a Protestant to the College of Cardinals —the Chief Justice's first choice was John W. Davis, an eminent Wall Street lawyer who had been Woodrow Wilson's ambassador to England. When Davis declined to be a candidate, Taft, with Van Devanter's help, turned to Pierce Butler and conducted a long, vigorous, and ultimately successful campaign to get him appointed.

In his choice of a Democrat, Taft was hardly indulging starry-eyed, bipartisan idealism. He wanted a conservative as rock-ribbed as himself and realized full well that American party labels are often unreliable indications of ideology. Pierce Butler shared Taft's basic values, and Taft knew it. Butler was opposed to government regulation of business, perhaps even more than Taft himself. Like the Chief, Butler valued teamwork on the Court and his ready wit enabled him to get along well with his colleagues. As he wrote on the back of one of Justice Stone's slip opinions:

> I voted to reverse. While this sustains your conclusion to affirm, I still think reversal would be better. But I shall in silence acquiesce. Dissents seldom aid in the right development or statement of the law. They often do harm. For myself I say: "Lead us not into temptation."[28]

Edward Terry Sanford was the eighth judge in seniority on the Taft Court. Born in Knox, Tennessee just after General Lee's surrender at Appomattox, he had gone to Harvard Law School and had returned to practice law in his home state. In 1907 he had worked for President Roosevelt as an Assistant Attorney General, and Roosevelt had appointed him a federal district judge in 1908.

In the winter of 1922–23, with Justice Mahlon Pitney's retirement pending, the Chief Justice began to cast about for a promising new colleague. His first choice was Judge Charles Hough, a federal judge on the Circuit Court for the Second Circuit; but Harding thought Hough, who was then sixty-five, too old, and seemed to be leaning toward a liberal like Benjamin Cardozo or Learned Hand. Taft, of course, was horrified, and he again waged a vigorous campaign with the President, the Attorney General, the Chairman of the Finance Committee of the Republican National Committee, and any potentially influential person who would listen (and many who would not), warning against putting a man on the Court who would "herd with Brandeis."[29]

As a compromise candidate Attorney General Daugherty suggested Sanford. A Republican from a southern state and the brother of the editor of one of the most important—and one of the very few—GOP newspapers in the South, Sanford was politically acceptable in high Republican party circles. An experienced judge of conservative bent, he was also acceptable to the Chief Justice. Taft, however, had no illusions about Sanford's professional abilities and intellectual stamina. The Chief had been warned by Charles C. Burlingham, one of the leaders of the New York bar, that Sanford was "vacillating and fussy," something of "a granny"; and Taft candidly confessed that Sanford was not "the strongest man," but he so much preferred him to a liberal "that I would now be glad to have him appointed."[30]

Burlingham's estimate of Sanford had been essentially correct. He was devoted to the Court and its Chief, honest, pleasant, and intelligent, and met minimum professional standards; but that was about all that could be said. Harold Laski once remarked that Sanford was "amiable" but not "eminent,"[31] the sort of man who "made a virtue of dullness."[32] Soon after coming to the bench he let Washington social life take up too much of his time and fell behind in his judicial labors, but even after he had learned this lesson his contribution to the work of the Court was never significant, except to supply an added vote for the constitutional views of his chief.

The junior member of the Taft Court was Harlan Fiske Stone, former professor and dean of the law school of Columbia University, whom President Coolidge had summoned from a Wall Street practice to come to Washington as Attorney General and clean up the Harding–Daugherty scandals in the Justice Department. In late 1924, after he had asked Justice Joseph McKenna to retire because of failing health and intellectual acumen, the Chief Justice called at the White House and strongly urged the President to appoint Stone to the next vacancy. In later years Stone doubted the efficacy of Taft's intervention, but one may surmise that the support of the Chief Justice of the United States did not hurt Stone's chances of going to the Court.

In any event, Taft backed Stone because he thought the Attorney General to be a staunch conservative, and, at the time he was appointed, he was. But Stone had an open mind, and the warm friendship and intellectual brilliance of Holmes and Brandeis attracted him toward the liberal wing of the Court on both economic and civil liberties issues. Taft tried for a time to woo Stone back into the conservative camp, but eventually concluded that Stone had become as hopelessly progressive as Brandeis.

In many ways the justices of the Taft Court represented a geographical and religious cross-section of American society. Sutherland and Van Devanter came from the West; Taft and Butler, from the Midwest; Holmes, Brandeis, and Stone, from the Northeast; McReynolds and Sanford, from the South. Holmes was an agnostic; Brandeis, a Jew; Butler, a Catholic; Taft, a Unitarian. All the rest were, formally at least, Protestants. Socially and ethnically, however, the Court's membership was not representative of American society. All of the justices were from northern European stock —English, Irish, Dutch, Scotch—except for Brandeis, whose parents had been Bohemian immigrants. With the exception of Pierce Butler, the justices came from upper-middle-class or upper-class families. Professionally, all were lawyers and able ones, though their abilities ranged from mere competence to genius. In addition, every member of the Court, with the possible exception of Holmes, had had some political experience before coming to the bench. Only Brandeis had not held public office, and he had acted both before and after his appointment as an intimate adviser to President Wilson. Thus each of the justices could bring to bear on his work not only technical legal knowledge, but also broad experience in public affairs.

If Olmstead's case had involved merely government regulation of business—and in a sense, of course, this question was involved—the reaction of the justices could have been accurately predicted. But adoption of the prohibition amendment had put Olmstead's business activities outside the legal pale. His case thus involved not property but other civil rights allegedly protected by the Fourth and Fifth Amendments.

Since the Court in the 1920s decided relatively few civil liberties controversies, it would have been far harder to predict how the justices would respond to Olmstead's arguments. Logically, the conservatives might have voted against government interference with individual rights, and the liberals might have tolerated official action. This sort of consistency, however, assumes that each justice valued property rights equally with other rights. The actual facts were very different; each justice had a value hierarchy, not a system of equal values. The same conservatives who felt that minimum wage laws for women or laws against child labor violated the natural freedom necessary for the good life were frequently unmoved by government abridgments of free speech, denials of fair trials, or racial discrimination. On the other hand, the liberals who were perfectly willing to see government officials experiment with property rights shuddered at the thought of government experimentation with other rights.

Although originally opposed to adoption of the Eighteenth Amendment, Taft was appalled at the lawlessness of the 1920s and publicly advocated more strenuous enforcement of the Volstead Act. In an interview he gave in 1926 to a writer for *Collier's* magazine, the Chief Justice echoed statements he had made before going to the White House: the public should not be overscrupulous about the methods police must use to catch criminals.[33] Thus, Olmstead's counsel probably crossed off the Chief's vote and Justice Department lawyers probably marked it as a sure thing.

Van Devanter had spoken and written little about civil liberties. The main clue to his reaction would be his personal and ideological propinquity to the Chief Justice. So, too, would it have been with Sanford, though the lines of influence here ran from Taft to Sanford and were not, as with Taft and Van Devanter, reciprocal.

At the other extreme from Taft were Brandeis and Stone. In 1890, with his law partner, Samuel Warren, Brandeis had written what has become a classic article defending the right of privacy against interference by government officials and nosy neighbors.[34] It was not likely that the author of that article would be sympathetic to wiretapping. Nor was it likely that Stone, who as Attorney General had forbidden Justice Department officials to use wiretapping because he considered it unethical conduct, would be sympathetic to electronic eavesdropping.

Holmes, McReynolds, Sutherland, and Butler would have posed difficult questions for one interested in predicting the outcome of the case. Holmes, like Brandeis and Stone, was far more suspicious of government regulation of civil rights than of property rights; but Holmes was also a toughminded Boston Brahmin who understood little and concerned himself less about people like Roy Olmstead, Jeremiah Finch, and their business associates. Holmes had, for instance, written the opinion of the Court upholding the imprisonment of the Socialist leader Eugene Debs for making pacifist statements during World War I.[35]

McReynolds was simply too ornery to be predictable. He usually voted against civil liberties claims, but his own desire to be let alone might carry him over into the civil libertarian camp, at least on the wiretapping issue. Sutherland's commitment here was also ambiguous. He rarely joined in an opinion upholding freedom of speech, and he did join in a dissent against a decision to reverse a conviction obtained at a trial which had been conducted in an atmosphere of mob rule.[36] In later years, however, he would write an opinion for the Court holding for the first time in Supreme Court history that in certain kinds of cases, state governments would have to supply a lawyer for an indigent defendant.[37]

The question is still open today as to how much of a civil libertarian Pierce Butler was. Some of the opposition to his appointment to the Court had come from people who charged that, as a regent of the University of Minnesota, he had run roughshod over the rights of pacifist faculty members during World War I. Over his whole career his votes on the Court were not always consistent. At times he was the staunchest defender among the justices of civil liberties claims; at other times he evinced little concern for such freedoms.[38] Before the Olmstead case, however, there was little indication how Butler would react, as a judge, to the wiretapping issue.

Given the predisposition of Taft and probably Van Devanter and Sanford to choose police efficiency over rights of privacy, and the opposite preference of Brandeis and Stone, the fate of Roy Olmstead and his associates rested in large part on the ability of opposing counsel to sway Holmes, McReynolds, Sutherland, and Butler. Equally important, the fate of the Olmstead defendants rested on the abilities of the opposing justices to influence one another as well as their uncommitted brethren. In this sort of situation, Taft would have a real advantage, especially if he could unite his personal charm and skill as presiding officer with Van Devanter's erudition.

CHAPTER

7

The Justices Deliberate

Passage of the 1925 judiciary act had enabled the justices to clear up most of their backlog of cases, and the Clerk of the Court set Monday, February 20, 1928, as the day for oral argument in *Olmstead* v. *United States*. Since the basic issue of the constitutionality of wiretapping had first been raised in pretrial maneuvering almost three years earlier and had appeared time and again at the trial and appellate proceedings, one would have expected that lawyers on both sides would have long since polished their fundamental arguments to a fine sheen. Such, however, was not the case. Supreme Court justices have often complained—sometimes bitterly—of the generally poor quality of argument before them, and counsel in the Olmstead litigation were either unable or unwilling to rise above minimal standards.

A mediocre performance from an attorney who has never previously appeared before the Supreme Court is understandable, and although Vandeveer and Finch each brought in two additional Seattle lawyers and one of the other defendants had by now hired a seventh attorney, none of these counsel was accustomed to Supreme Court practice. Petitioners' briefs, however, certainly were written no more poorly than those of the Justice Department, and it is less common to have a faulty performance from the staff of the Solicitor General.

One possible explanation for the low quality of the government's brief may have been the division among responsible officials on the legitimacy of wiretapping. It will be recalled that the Treasury Department, which was still responsible for the enforcement of prohibition, officially disapproved of wiretapping. The Justice Department, following Stone's policy, also disapproved of this tactic. Yet prohibition agents had tapped telephones, a U.S. Attorney had prosecuted on the basis of evidence so obtained, a federal judge had allowed such evidence, and a jury had returned a verdict of guilty.

Because of this policy conflict, the government's brief had to be carefully phrased not to defend wiretapping as a moral or a desirable policy, but solely as a policy constitutionally permissible, however unpleasant. The *Brief for the United States* frankly admitted the opposition to wiretapping by the Treasury and Justice departments, but went on to state:

> No other recent case in the federal courts has come to our attention in which officers of the United States have resorted to it. The question here is not one of governmental or departmental policy, but of constitutional law.

Because of the implications of the Olmstead case, high Justice Department officials had been watching the litigation from its early stages. Observers from the capital had been present throughout the trial, and Mrs. Mabel Willebrant, Assistant Attorney General in charge of all Volstead Act prosecutions, had come to Seattle to watch part of the proceedings. She and William Mitchell, Solicitor General of the United States, had signed the brief for the United States asking the Court to deny certiorari, and the brief on the merits had been signed by Michael J. Doherty, Special Assistant to the Attorney General, and by the Solicitor General himself. (Mitchell and Doherty, incidentally, had been Pierce Butler's law partners in Minnesota, and Mitchell had been appointed Solicitor General in large part through the intercession of Taft. One might suspect that Taft's interest in Mitchell had been nourished by Butler, and that Mitchell, too, remembered his friends when he was in power.)

Essentially, petitioners reasserted their earlier arguments that wiretapping was a violation of the Fifth Amendment's protection against self-incrimination* and the Fourth Amendment's protection of privacy. In addition, petitioners went beyond the expressed limits of the grant of certiorari and asserted that wiretapping was a crime in Washington and therefore under the *Weeks* rule should not be used in a federal court.

In reply the Department of Justice made three points. First, under the common law the way in which evidence was obtained had no bearing on its admissibility. The *Weeks* rule modified the common law only to the extent of excluding evidence obtained in violation of the Fourth Amendment. The issue of the criminality of wiretapping was thus irrelevant. Second, the Fourth Amendment protects against physical invasions of property. It had never been held to exclude evidence overheard by a person who was not trespassing. One cannot "search" or "seize" a conversation, and the Constitution forbade only unreasonable searches and seizures. If the Fourth Amendment were interpreted in its literal sense, Doherty

* The relevant part of the Fifth Amendment provides: "nor shall [any person] be compelled in any criminal case to be a witness against himself. . . ." For the Fourth Amendment, see above, p. 26n.

and Mitchell contended, "it does not seem possible to include within its meaning anything other than tangible personal property or extend it to include a telephone conversation or any intangible right of privacy. . . ." Third, the Department of Justice maintained that there was even less reason to find an invasion of Fifth Amendment rights. No one had coerced or induced Olmstead and the others to talk on the telephone. They had done so of their own free will, without fear of punishment or promise of reward.

Only one brief in the case met high professional standards. A group of telephone companies, including the Pacific Telephone and Telegraph Company, which serviced Seattle, asked and received permission to present a brief as *amicus curiae*, that is, "friend of the court." It frequently happens that a person or association not actually and immediately involved in a particular suit will have legal interests that may be directly affected by the outcome of the case. Sometimes a court will invite such persons to appear and present their views as interested parties. A later Supreme Court, for instance, before handing down its implementing order in the school segregation cases was, in 1954, to invite attorneys general from all southern states to file briefs. It is more common, however, for interested parties to petition the Court to be allowed to speak.

The telephone companies argued strenuously against the government and on behalf of Olmstead. It was clear that their own interests were involved and, as good lawyers always do, counsel for the phone companies linked their clients' interests with those of the general public. Reminding the Court that twenty-three states made it a crime to tap telephone lines, the companies asserted:

> The function of a telephone system in our modern economy is, so far as reasonably practicable, to

> enable any two persons at a distance to converse privately with each other as they might do if both were personally present in the privacy of the home or office of either one. When the lines of "two parties" are connected with the central office, they are intended to be devoted to their exclusive use, and in that sense to be turned over to the exclusive possession, of the parties. A third person who taps the lines violates the property rights of both persons then using the telephone, and of the telephone company as well.

To bolster this last point, counsel cited a 1918 Supreme Court decision holding that International News Service had violated the property rights of the Associated Press in pirating news sent out over telegraph lines to other Associated Press agents.[1]

The telephone companies then turned their legal guns on the government's contention that there could be no "seizure" of a conversation:

> [T]his is purely a superficial view, which puts the letter above the spirit and intent of the law. The "privacy of life" and the liberty of the citizen have been invaded. And, in the second place, we do not understand that seizure is a necessary element to constitute the offense. An unreasonable search alone violates the fourth amendment. It is enough that the federal officer has made an unreasonable search, within the meaning of the fourth amendment, and has thereby unlawfully *obtained* evidence. The evidence so obtained is excluded on the provisions of the fifth amendment.

It is at oral argument that the justices try to obtain the kind of information and discussion they do not receive in the briefs. Normally each side has an hour or less to present its case. Counsel stands at a lectern facing the nine justices behind their huge, polished mahogany desk. Nowadays, a white light flashes on the lectern to warn the attorney when five minutes of his time are remaining; when a red light goes on, he must stop. In the 1920s, however, an attorney had to keep track of his own time, or risk annoying the Court by asking the Chief Justice how many minutes were left. The lawyer must be frugal with his time, because the justices are miserly with theirs. The story has been told that Chief Justice Hughes once cut off an eminent lawyer in the middle of the word "if."

In the early days of the Republic, the justices, like most Americans, enjoyed formal oratory. Daniel Webster would speak for several days, elegantly, passionately pleading his case. More recently, the justices prefer a dialogue—or whatever is the proper term for a discussion in which nine are pitted against one. The emphasis in oral argument is on informality. Pages run in and out of the courtroom, carrying books, records, and briefs for the justices to check a point of law or question of fact. The justices often talk to each other or scribble notes which are passed up and down the bench. Indeed, the informality of the justices, in contrast to the almost pompous dignity of the courtroom itself, has been offensive to some people. In the 1890s, when he was Solicitor General Taft, the future Chief Justice complained: "I have difficulty in holding the attention of the court. They seem to think when I begin to talk that that is a good chance to read all the letters that have been waiting for some time, to eat lunch,* and to devote their atten-

* It was not until sometime during the Chief Justiceship of Melville Weston Fuller, around the turn of the century, that the justices took time out for lunch. Before that each justice, when he became hungry, would retire behind a screen and eat, sandwiching oral argument with a snack.

tion to correcting proof, and other matters that have been delayed until my speech."[2]

Perhaps Taft's last word revealed the source of his trouble. With their time severely limited and their need for knowledge enormous, the justices tend to rebel against speech-making. They prefer that an attorney offer, as tersely as possible, an outline of his case. Then, with the issues sharply delineated, the justices like to ply the lawyer with questions as fast as he can answer them —and sometimes faster, since it is not unusual for two or three justices to ask questions simultaneously. This judicial search for factual knowledge and jurisprudential light can be a most trying experience for counsel, whose job it is to inform and enlighten, and more than one able lawyer has faltered in his efforts to keep up with nine minds racing down different and equally learned paths. Solicitor General Stanley Reed, who later went to the Court himself, once fainted dead away from exhaustion after oral argument, and it is not uncommon for an attorney before the Court to be stricken suddenly with a most unlawyer-like malady, muteness.

At its best, oral argument before the Supreme Court is an exhilarating though enervating experience for lawyers, justices, and spectators. At its worst, it resembles a seminar in which the main participants are unprepared and the rest drowsy. When the Court is quiet it may be evidence of great respect for counsel. The justices, for instance, allowed John W. Davis, the *doyen* of the Supreme Court bar, to present almost uninterrupted his argument for South Carolina in the school segregation cases. More often, silence indicates that the justices think the case is trivial—and probably wish they had never granted certiorari—or that the lawyer is making a complete mess of things. To keep awake during such periods, some justices rock vigorously to and fro in their high-backed, leather chairs; others stare at the ceiling and catch up on their meditations; others outline a possible opinion in this or another case. Holmes had his own little ways of demonstrating displeasure with counsel. As he grew older he usually napped during oral argument, though typically he first sketched a coherent outline of what the lawyer was going to say. When the old gentleman found a presentation particularly bad, he might frequently and ostentatiously consult his watch. Once after an attorney, who had been talking for most of his allotted time, preened himself and sternly warned the Court that he was now coming to the main point of his argument, Holmes, who had been dozing, snapped to attention, looked at his watch, and said audibly: "Oh, Christ!" Then the great judge resumed his nap.

The oral argument in *Olmstead* v. *United States* was in the grand rather than the turgid style. Hardly had the first counsel for petitioners begun to speak when he was interrupted by a series of inquiries from the bench. For the government, Michael Doherty faced a similar barrage of rapid-fire questions. Brandeis was especially dogged in his interrogation. He kept returning to the question whether prohibition agents had not committed greater violations of privacy by appropriating entire conversations than they would have by seizing specific documents. Doherty candidly admitted that he thought that wiretapping was the more serious violation of privacy. But, he added, it was not the kind of violation the Constitution forbade, and it was this issue only which was before the Court.

An eye-witness described the courtroom scene:

> So sharp and persistent were the questions from the bench that neither Frank R. Jeffrey of Seattle, who made the closing argument for the defendants, nor Michael J. Doherty . . . was able to follow any sustained line of argument very far. Renewed

efforts by the attorneys to "get up steam" failed time after time because of pointed interruptions from the bench, most of them of a challenging character.[3]

The *Olmstead* argument had begun late Monday afternoon. Promptly at 4:30 Taft adjourned the Court, and argument continued at noon on Tuesday. As soon as the harassed and exhausted lawyers had completed their presentations, the Chief Justice called for argument in the next case on the docket. As far as the outside world was concerned *Olmstead* v. *United States* now dropped into a silent void. Nothing would be heard of it again outside the Court until days or weeks or months later when the justices would announce their decision.

Within the Court, however, much would be heard and much more said about Olmstead's problems. On Saturday, February 25, 1928, the justices met for their weekly conference to discuss and vote on the cases just argued. At these conferences the Chief Justice presides. He usually opens the discussion on a particular case with a short summary of the facts and states his own views about the proper decision. Then, in order of seniority, each associate justice offers his views. When the Chief Justice feels that the discussion has played itself out or that the press of time forces the Court to move on, he calls for a vote. The justices vote in reverse order of seniority, the most recently appointed associate justice first, the Chief last.

These conferences are secret and no one except the justices is admitted to the room. Each justice brings to the conference whatever papers he wishes to use to refresh his memory and his docket book, a large volume bound in red leather and kept locked when not in actual use. In it the justice records his votes and those of his colleagues. Although some justices have taken notes of what is said in conference—perhaps to aid them in writing opinions, perhaps as a record for posterity—as of June 1965 only two sets of such notes covering a large number of cases have been available to all scholars: those of Justice Frank Murphy, who sat on the Court from 1939 to 1949, and Harold H. Burton, who served from 1949 to 1958. As one would suspect, even these notes do not cover all the cases in which Murphy and Burton participated, and at best they are elliptical summaries rather than verbatim accounts of what was said. From copies of letters and memoranda in the Taft papers, however, it is possible to reconstruct the general outline of what went on at the *Olmstead* conference.

From his later opinion and his earlier statements warning against coddling criminals, it would be expected that Taft spoke in favor of affirming the convictions. He probably argued that wiretapping did not violate the Fourth Amendment because there was no invasion of property rights. Holmes, the senior associate justice, agreed reluctantly. He did not like wiretapping, but he thought it neither illegal nor unconstitutional. Van Devanter also agreed with the Chief. McReynolds was next and he probably said very few words—undoubtedly most of them caustic—but went along with the preceding justices.

It was Brandeis who put forth the first negative view, and one can imagine him putting it with all the strength of his massive talents as an advocate. He thought wiretapping was an invasion of the right to privacy, a right whose protection was the cardinal purpose of the Fourth Amendment. Moreover, wiretapping was certainly illegal in the state of Washington. Either at this point or somewhat later, Holmes interrupted and asked Brandeis why he had said wiretapping was illegal. Brandeis explained that it was a misdemeanor under Washington law. Holmes then stated that this fact changed his view. He did not believe that evidence obtained by crime could be used in a federal court.

Sutherland was the next senior judge. Since he had been ill much of that term, it is possible that he did not attend the conference, or even hear oral argument.[4] When he could not attend a conference, he would leave his votes with Taft to cast for him. In any event, Sutherland agreed with the Chief Justice on the merits of this case. Pierce Butler was next. Despite his close friendship with the Chief Justice, he had to register disagreement. For somewhat different reasons than those advanced by Brandeis, Butler felt that prohibition agents had violated the Constitution. Sanford then spoke and agreed with Taft. Last was Stone, the junior justice, and he came out in favor of the position Brandeis had stated.

When the voting was completed, the decision was five to four to affirm the conviction. The Chief Justice, if he votes with the majority, assigns the task of writing the opinion of the Court to himself or to one of the justices who voted with him. (If the Chief is in the minority, the senior associate justice in the majority assigns the opinion.) In making these assignments the Chief Justice has to weigh a number of factors: the workload of each justice, the peculiar expertise and taste of the individual members of the Court, and, of course, the substantive views of each potential writer. This last factor operates in several ways. First, if he thinks the case important, the Chief Justice would like the opinion to conform to his own views. Second, and this consideration may well conflict with the first, he wants an opinion that will unite the Court or, at least, cause the minimum division. Generally speaking, a 6–3 opinion carries more weight than one that is 5–4, a 7–2 more than a 6–3, and so on. Yet there is a price for additional votes which a policy-oriented justice would probably not be willing to pay, and a strong opinion, even if supported only by five or six justices, will probably have greater impact than a wishy-washy unanimous expression.

Taft was able to balance these considerations by assigning the *Olmstead* opinion to himself. Actually, he had little choice. Sutherland's health would not allow him to take on another opinion in a difficult case. Van Devanter wrote too slowly to be trusted to get the opinion out before the end of the term, and failure to hand down the decision before then would probably entail reargument the next term. McReynolds' surliness would be likely to weld the dissenters together and probably produce an acrimonious public debate, something Taft abhorred. Sanford was the only other alternative, and the Chief did not have faith in his ability to write an opinion in a case of this significance.

Depending on their inclinations and workload, the dissenters may agree to have one of their number prepare an opinion for the group, or each may decide to try his own hand. Alternatively, a justice may simply record his vote without offering an explanation. No matter which course the dissenters originally agree upon, no justice is obliged to put his name to an opinion that does not meet his full approval. This rule applies to the majority as well, and causes more difficult problems since, for an opinion to be labeled as that of the Court, at least five justices (or a majority of those sitting in a case) must sign it.

Getting five strong-willed and individualistic judges to agree on a single, closely reasoned statement of their views demands of the writer not only professional knowledge and literary skill, but also some diplomatic talents. He must be able to accommodate his writing style and substantive ideas to those of his colleagues and still retain the essence of his own views. Typically, the process of securing majority agreement in an important case is one of negotiation, even bargaining.[5] The opinion writer's task is made all the more arduous because a concession that wins one justice—perhaps a member of the minority who is willing to suppress his dissent if the majority changes the wording of the opinion—may at the same time lose another vote.

The mechanics of the intra-Court process are actually rather simple. The opinion writer, with the aid of his law clerks, gets the opinion in the shape he thinks most likely to gain approval. Then he sends it to the printer. When this draft is returned (in this form it is called a "slip opinion") the justice sends a copy to each member of the majority. He may also send copies to the dissenters at this time, or wait until the majority has reached some sort of consensus; but he will give the dissenters ample opportunity to read, think over, and, if they wish, reply to what the majority will say. When a justice receives a slip opinion, protocol requires him to give it first priority in his time schedule. If he approves it, he simply says so on the back of the last page. A terse "I agree" is common, though a justice may express his consent with more flair. Holmes was particularly good at penning eloquent little notes on slip opinions. As he wrote on the back of one of Taft's: "I cling to my preceptor's hand and follow him through the dark passages to the light."[6]

Very often, however, a justice has some doubts. If these are minor he may note them in the margins of the slip opinion. If they are involved, he will usually attach a memorandum with a full explanation. Sometimes a justice will send a memorandum in the form of a draft opinion of his own so that the official writer will get the flavor of his comments. Such a memorandum serves also as a deft warning that the doubter is prepared to leave the majority and strike out on his own. It is always clearly understood that if suggested changes are not made, or some compromise reached, the opinion writer risks the loss of the doubter's vote and possibly of his majority. Where majority agreement seems impossible the writer reports back to the Chief Justice, who may reassign the opinion to another justice or, if the Court appears hopelessly divided, simply urge that the case be decided without an institutional opinion, each justice being at liberty to write or join in individual expressions of views.

The dissenters follow much the same procedure as the majority, though they may legitimately decide to see the finished product of the majority before beginning to write. If they decide on the latter course, they are under an obligation to work quickly lest the decision be delayed beyond the end of the term. When the minority opinion or opinions are completed, copies are sent to members of the majority; then the author of the Court's opinion may decide—or be asked by other members of the majority—to make some changes to answer the minority. Or another member of the majority may decide to file a separate opinion rebutting the dissenter. The minority in its turn, having read the new version of the Court's opinion and/or the concurring opinion, may amend its dissent. This process of debate, editing, and negotiation continues until both sides are satisfied. Obviously it can be a long process. When it is done, the author of the majority opinion so informs the Chief Justice, who announces at the next conference that, if there is nothing further to be said, the decision will be handed down as soon as is convenient.*

It was not until the last week in May that Taft had a draft of his opinion in condition to circulate. Since his

* One of the reasons behind the Court's change in 1965 to announcing decisions on days other than Monday was to allow the news media to analyze opinions with greater care and accuracy than had been possible when perhaps a dozen important cases were disposed of on a single day. It is not improbable, therefore, that the justices deliberately delay the publication of some decisions.

doctor had told him not to return to the Court until the following October, Sutherland had given his consent to any opinion Taft might write. Sutherland's absence meant that Taft had only three others to please; but, since he wanted to adjourn the Court by the first Monday in June, majority agreement had to be secured quickly. Knowing that McReynolds had a penchant for brief opinions, Taft tried to keep his writing parsimonious—a most difficult task for one inclined to indirect phrasing. But, within a few days of circulation, each of the three had expressed general agreement, though McReynolds had returned a detailed memorandum suggesting numerous changes.[7] Meanwhile, Brandeis had circulated a memorandum outlining the form his dissent would take, and to answer it Taft added a paragraph to his opinion stressing that the historical purpose of the Fourth Amendment was to protect physical property—homes, papers, and personal effects—and that the cases Brandeis cited were all to this effect.

In addition to matters of substance, Brandeis' draft had raised a serious problem of procedure for the Chief Justice. In spite of the limitation on the grant of certiorari to the constitutional question, Brandeis, as at conference, had reasoned that wiretapping evidence was also inadmissible because it had been obtained in violation of Washington law. In the last few years, Taft, by his own admission, had felt his intellectual powers ebbing, and he was inclined to see his conservative jurisprudence more and more threatened by Brandeis. Now the Chief was angry at what he believed was unethical conduct in Brandeis' bringing up a point of law excluded from consideration. Pierce Butler, though among the dissenters, was no less irritated and told Taft that the Court should not allow Brandeis to use the statutory grounds in his opinions—though Butler did not explain how a Chief Justice might curb a dissenting justice's free speech.

In the privacy of his family, Taft gave full vent to his anger, but among his colleagues he was conciliatory, saying they might as well let the matter drop, especially since Holmes was taking the same line. Sanford, however, and perhaps Van Devanter and McReynolds, were less willing to turn the other cheek and wanted to call attention to what they, too, considered a breach of judicial etiquette. As he sometimes did when he needed to secure rapid agreement, Taft invited the other three majority justices to his home on Sunday morning to discuss strategy. At this "rump conference," Taft gave in and inserted in his opinion a paragraph emphasizing the limited nature of the grant of certiorari. Pierce Butler also opened his dissenting opinion with a similar statement.

The minority justices were at work at the same time the majority justices were putting their opinion together. As had been indicated, Pierce Butler struck out alone, sincerely unhappy to find himself aligned against Taft in the company of Holmes and Brandeis. Indeed, Butler had delayed writing until the majority opinion had been prepared, hoping there might be some way in which he could join his usual company.

Brandeis undertook the task of writing for the other dissenters and had a complete draft ready in the form of a memorandum a full two months ahead of Taft. Brandeis based his opinion on two independent grounds: (1) wiretapping violated the Fourth Amendment; and (2) it was a state crime. Holmes was unsure of the first ground, as he had been at conference, but agreed with the second. In his usual fashion the old justice fired off a succinct, crisply worded statement explaining his views. Brandeis, seeing that their differences were major and not wishing to modify or conceal his own constitutional views, urged Holmes to publish his explanation as a separate dissent. Holmes at first thought he should not, but later gave in.[8]

When Stone read Brandeis' opinion, he agreed to join in it, but with one reservation and one suggestion for an addition. He objected to the inclusion of an analogy to the "doctrine of clean hands" in equity,* under which a court refuses to assist a litigant unless he himself is innocent of wrongdoing. The addition Stone wanted was an explicit statement that it was equally wrong for federal officers to violate state law to obtain evidence as to violate the Constitution.[9] Brandeis retained the "clean hands" analogy, but he—and Holmes—readily adopted the second point. Stone gladly joined in both dissents and wrote a paragraph of his own answering the comments of the Chief Justice and Butler about the grant of certiorari.

Taft said he always approached a Saturday confer-

* Law dictionaries usually describe equity as a system of jurisprudence distinct from the common law, but this definition takes on real meaning only in a historical context. In its early stages the common law went through a period of extreme rigidity. Judges simply turned away litigants whose claims could not be met by the issuance of one of a small group of technical writs or orders. These litigants began appealing to the king for justice, and by the fourteenth century such petitions were regularly being referred to the king's chancellor for decision. Gradually a judicial system parallel to that of the common law courts grew up, called courts of chancery or equity, in which procedure was more simple and remedies more flexible than in the common law tribunals. The purpose was to do justice without slavish adherence to precedent or strict observance of technicalities. Over the centuries equity and common law have influenced one another, so that nowadays the common law is no longer so rigid, and equity decisions depend on more than the judge's idiosyncratic notions of justice. Today in Great Britain and most of the United States, courts of law and equity are not separate institutions; rather one court usually has two kinds of procedure. To invoke the more flexible equity jurisdiction of a court, however, a litigant must first show that he has no remedy at law.

ence with his brethren with much the same trepidation as an undergraduate going into an examination, and he was particularly concerned that the final discussion of the Olmstead case might be acrimonious. He was, however, certain that his position was the right one. On the morning of June 2, 1928, the Chief wrote his brother: "We go for the last Conference of the Court . . . this morning, and we are going to have a divided Court on a very contested case. The decision may bring down, and probably will, the condemnation of idealists and others, but I am convinced that it is the law."

At the conference Taft announced that the decision would be published the following Monday if there were no objections. The other justices agreed, apparently without further discussion. At high noon on Monday, June 4, the Chief Justice stated that the first order of business was the decision in *Olmstead* v. *United States*. He then began to read his opinion. When Taft was done, first Holmes, then Brandeis, then Butler and Stone read theirs. Olmstead had had his last day in court.[10]

CHAPTER

8

The Justices Speak*

ROY OLMSTEAD, Jerry L. Finch, Clarence G. Healy, Cliff Maurice, Tom Nakagawa, Edward Engdahl, Myer Berg, John Earl, and Francis Richard Brown, Petitioners

v.

UNITED STATES OF AMERICA (No. 493)

CHARLES S. GREEN, Emory A. Kern, Z. J. Hendrick, Edward Erickson, William P. Smith, David Trotsky, Louis O. Gilliam, Clyde Thompson, and B. G. Ward, Petitioners

v.

UNITED STATES OF AMERICA (No. 532)

EDWARD H. MCINNIS, Petitioner

v.

UNITED STATES OF AMERICA (No. 533)

Mr. Chief Justice TAFT delivered the opinion of the Court. . . .

* The text of this chapter consists entirely of material drawn from the Supreme Court opinions in *Olmstead* v. *United States*.

It will be helpful to consider the chief cases in this Court which bear upon the construction of these Amendments.

Boyd v. *United States*[1] . . . was a cause of seizure and forfeiture against thirty-five cases of plate glass, which charged that the owner and importer, with intent to defraud the revenue, made an entry of the imported merchandise by means of a fraudulent or false invoice. It became important to show the quantity and value of glass contained in twenty-nine cases previously imported. The fifth section of the Act of June 22, 1874, provided that in cases not criminal under the revenue laws, the United States Attorney, whenever he thought an invoice, belonging to the defendant, would tend to prove an allegation made by the United States, might by a written motion describing the invoice and setting forth the allegation which he expected to prove, secure a notice from the court to the defendant to produce the invoice, and if the defendant refused to produce it, the allegations stated in the motion should be taken as confessed, but if produced, the United States Attorney should be permitted, under the direction of the court, to make an examination of the invoice, and might offer the same in evidence. . . .

The court held the Act of 1874 repugnant to the Fourth and Fifth Amendments. As to the Fourth Amendment, Justice Bradley said:

". . . it is contended that, whatever might have been alleged against the constitutionality of the acts of 1863 and 1867, that of 1874 . . . is free from constitutional objection because it does not authorize the search and seizure of books and papers, but only requires the defendant or claimant to produce them. That is so; but it declares that if he does not produce them, the allegations which it is affirmed they will prove shall be taken as confessed. This is tantamount to compelling their production; for the prosecuting attorney will always be sure to state the evidence expected to be derived from them as strongly as the case will admit of. It is true that certain aggravating incidents of actual search and seizure, such as forcible entry into a man's house and searching amongst his papers, are wanting . . . but it accomplishes the substantial object of those acts in forcing from a party evidence against himself. It is our opinion, therefore, that a compulsory production of a man's private papers to establish a criminal charge against him, or to forfeit his property, is within the scope of the Fourth Amendment to the Constitution, in all cases in which a search and seizure would be; because it is a material ingredient, and effects the sole object and purpose of search and seizure." . . .

The next case, and perhaps the most important, is *Weeks* v. *United States*[2] . . .—a conviction for using the mails to transmit coupons or tickets in a lottery enterprise. The defendant was arrested by a police officer without a warrant. After his arrest other police officers and the United States marshal went to his house, got the key from a neighbor, entered the defendant's room and searched it, and took possession of various papers and articles. Neither the marshal nor the police officers had a search warrant. . . . This court held that such taking of papers by an official of the United States, acting under color of his office, was in violation of the constitutional rights of the defendant, and . . . that by permitting their use upon the trial, the trial court erred.

The opinion cited with approval language of Mr. Justice Field in *Ex parte Jackson*,[3] . . . saying that the Fourth Amendment as a principle of protection was applicable to sealed letters and packages in the mail and that, consistently with it, such matter could only be opened and examined upon warrants issued on oath or affirmation particularly describing the thing to be seized.

In *Silverthorne Lumber Company* v. *United States,*[4] . . . the defendants were arrested at their homes and detained in custody. While so detained, representatives of the Government without authority went to the office of their company and seized all the books, papers and documents found there. . . . The court said:

"Thus the case is not that of knowledge acquired through the wrongful act of a stranger, but it must be assumed that the Government planned or at all events ratified the whole performance."

And it held that the illegal character of the original seizure characterized the entire proceeding and under the *Weeks* case the seized papers must be restored.

In *Amos* v. *United States,*[5] . . . the defendant was convicted of concealing whiskey on which the tax had not been paid. . . . A woman, who claimed to be his wife, was told by the revenue officers that they had come to search the premises for violation of the revenue law. She opened the door; they entered and found whiskey. Further searches in the house disclosed more. It was held that this action constituted a violation of the Fourth Amendment, and that the denial of the motion to restore the whiskey and to exclude the testimony was error.

In *Gouled* v. *The United States,*[6] . . . the facts were these: . . . Gouled was suspected of the crime. A private in the U.S. Army, pretending to make a friendly call on him, gained admission to his office and in his absence, without warrant of any character, seized and carried away several documents. One of these, belonging to Gouled, was delivered to the United States Attorney and by him introduced in evidence. . . . Admission of the paper was considered a violation of the Fourth Amendment. . . .

There is no room in the present case for applying the Fifth Amendment unless the Fourth Amendment was first violated. There was no evidence of compulsion to induce the defendants to talk over their many telephones. They were continually and voluntarily transacting business without knowledge of the interception. Our consideration must be confined to the Fourth Amendment.

The striking outcome of the *Weeks* case and those which followed it was the sweeping declaration that the Fourth Amendment, although not referring to or limiting the use of evidence in courts, really forbade its introduction if obtained by government officers through a violation of the Amendment. Theretofore many had supposed that under the ordinary common law rules, if the tendered evidence was pertinent, the method of obtaining it was unimportant. . . . But in the *Weeks* case, and those which followed, this Court decided with great emphasis, and established as the law for the federal courts, that the protection of the Fourth Amendment would be much impaired unless it was held that not only was the official violator of the rights under the Amendment subject to action at the suit of the injured defendant, but also that the evidence thereby obtained could not be received.

The well known historical purpose of the Fourth Amendment, directed against general warrants and writs of assistance, was to prevent the use of governmental force to search a man's house, his person, his papers and his effects; and to prevent their seizure against his will. This phase of the misuse of governmental power of compulsion is the emphasis of the opinion of the Court in the *Boyd* case. This appears too in the *Weeks* case, in the *Silverthorne* case and in the *Amos* case.

Gouled v. *United States* carried the inhibition against unreasonable searches and seizures to the extreme limit. Its authority is not to be enlarged by implication and must be confined to the precise state of facts disclosed by the record. . . . A stealthy entrance in such circumstances became the equivalent to an entry by force. There was actual entrance into the private quarters of defendant and the taking away of something tangible. Here we have testimony only of voluntary conversations secretly overheard.

The Amendment itself shows that the search is to be of material things—the person, the house, his papers or his effects. The description of the warrant necessary to make the proceeding lawful, is that it must specify the place to be searched and the person or *things* to be seized.

It is urged that the language of Mr. Justice Field in *Ex parte Jackson*, already quoted, offers an analogy to the interpretation of the Fourth Amendment in respect of wire tapping. But the analogy fails. The Fourth Amendment may have proper application to a sealed letter in the mail because of the constitutional provision for the Post Office Department and the relations between the Government and those who pay to secure protection of their sealed letters. . . . It is plainly within the words of the Amendment to say that the unlawful rifling by a government agent of a sealed letter is a search and seizure of the sender's papers or effects. The letter is a paper, an effect, and in the custody of a Government that forbids carriage except under its protection.

The United States takes no such care of telegraph or telephone messages as of mailed sealed letters. The Amendment does not forbid what was done here. There was no searching. There was no seizure. The evidence was secured by the use of the sense of hearing and that only. There was no entry of the houses or offices of the defendants.

By the invention of the telephone, fifty years ago, and its application for the purpose of extending communica tions, one can talk with another at a far distant place. The language of the Amendment can not be extended and expanded to include telephone wires reaching to the whole world from the defendant's house or office. The intervening wires are not part of his house or office any more than are the highways along which they are stretched.

This Court in *Carroll* v. *United States*,[7] . . . declared: "The Fourth Amendment is to be construed in the light of what was deemed an unreasonable search and seizure when it was adopted and in a manner which will conserve public interests as well as the interests and rights of individual citizens."

. . . *Hester* v. *United States*[8] . . . held that the testimony of two officers of the law who trespassed on the defendant's land, concealed themselves one hundred yards away from his house and saw him come out and hand a bottle of whiskey to another, was not inadmissible. While there was a trespass, there was no search of person, house, papers or effects. . . .

Congress may of course protect the secrecy of telephone messages by making them, when intercepted, inadmissible in evidence in federal criminal trials, by direct legislation, and thus depart from the common law of evidence. But the courts may not adopt such a policy by attributing an enlarged and unusual meaning to the Fourth Amendment. The reasonable view is that one who installs in his house a telephone instrument with connecting wires intends to project his voice to those quite outside, and that the wires beyond his house and messages while passing over them are not within the protection of the Fourth Amendment. Here those who intercepted the projected voices were not in the house of either party to the conversation. . . .

What has been said disposes of the only question that

comes within the terms of our order granting certiorari in these cases. But some of our number, departing from that order, have concluded that there is merit in the twofold objection overruled in both courts below that evidence obtained through intercepting of telephone messages by government agents was inadmissible because the mode of obtaining it was unethical and a misdemeanor under the law of Washington. To avoid any misapprehension of our views of that objection we shall deal with it in both of its phases.

While a Territory, the English common law prevailed in Washington and thus continued after her admission in 1889. The rules of evidence in criminal cases in courts of the United States sitting there, consequently are those of the common law. . . .

The common law rule is that the admissibility of evidence is not affected by the illegality of the means by which it was obtained. . . . The common law rule must apply in the case at bar.

Nor can we, without the sanction of congressional enactment, subscribe to the suggestion that the courts have a discretion to exclude evidence, the admission of which is not unconstitutional, because unethically secured. This would be at variance with the common law doctrine generally supported by authority. There is no case that sustains, nor any recognized text book that gives color to such a view. . . . Evidence secured by such means has always been received.

A standard which would forbid the reception of evidence if obtained by other than nice ethical conduct by government officials would make society suffer and give criminals greater immunity than has been known heretofore. In the absence of controlling legislation by Congress, those who realize the difficulties in bringing offenders to justice may well deem it wise that the exclusion of evidence should be confined to cases where rights under the Constitution would be violated by admitting it.

The statute of Washington, adopted in 1909, provides . . . that:

"Every person . . . who shall intercept, read or in any manner interrupt or delay the sending of a message over any telegraph or telephone line . . . shall be guilty of a misdemeanor."

This statute does not declare that evidence obtained by such interception shall be inadmissible, and by the common law, already referred to, it would not be. . . . Whether the State of Washington may prosecute and punish federal officers violating this law and those whose messages were intercepted may sue them civilly is not before us. . . .

The judgments of the Circuit Court of Appeals are affirmed. The mandates will go down forthwith under Rule 31.

Affirmed.

MR. JUSTICE HOLMES:

My brother BRANDEIS has given this case so exhaustive an examination that I desire to add but a few words. While I do not deny it, I am not prepared to say that the penumbra of the Fourth and Fifth Amendments covers the defendant, although I fully agree that Courts are apt to err by sticking too closely to the words of a law where those words import a policy that goes beyond them. . . . But I think, as MR. JUSTICE BRANDEIS says, that apart from the Constitution the Government ought not to use evidence obtained and only obtainable by a criminal act. There is no body of precedents by which we are bound, and which confines us to logical deduction from established rules. Therefore we must consider the two objects of desire, both of which we cannot have, and make up our minds which to choose. It is desirable that criminals should be detected, and to that end that all available evidence should be used. It also is desirable that the Government should not itself foster and pay for other crimes, when they are the means by which the evidence is to be obtained. If it pays its officers for having got evidence by crime I do not see why it may not as well pay them for getting it in the same way, and I can attach no importance to protestations of disapproval if it knowingly accepts and pays and announces that in future it will pay for the fruits. We have to choose, and for my part I think it a less evil that some criminals should escape than that the Government should play an ignoble part.

For those who agree with me, no distinction can be taken between the Government as prosecutor and the Government as judge. If the existing code does not permit district attorneys to have a hand in such dirty business it does not permit the judge to allow such iniquities to succeed. . . . And if all that I have said so far be accepted it makes no difference that in this case wire tapping is made a crime by the law of the State, not by the law of the United States. It is true that a State cannot make rules of evidence for Courts of the United States, but the State has authority over the conduct in question, and I hardly think that the United States would appear to greater advantage when paying for an odious crime against State law than when inciting to the disregard of its own. I am aware of the often repeated statement that in a criminal proceeding the Court will not take notice of the manner in which papers offered in evidence have been obtained. But that somewhat rudimentary mode of disposing of the question has been overthrown by *Weeks v. United States*, . . . and the cases that have followed it. I have said that we are free to choose between two principles of policy. But if we are to confine ourselves to precedent and logic the reason for excluding evidence obtained by violating the Constitution seems to me logically to lead to excluding evidence obtained by a crime of the officers of the law.

MR. JUSTICE BRANDEIS, dissenting. . . .

"We must never forget," said Mr. Chief Justice Marshall in *McCulloch* v. *Maryland*,[9] . . . "that it is a constitution we are expounding." Since then, this Court has repeatedly sustained the exercise of power by Congress, under various clauses of that instrument, over objects of which the Fathers could not have dreamed. . . . We have likewise held that general limitations on the powers of Government, like those embodied in the due process clauses of the Fifth and Fourteenth Amendments, do not forbid the United States or the States from meeting modern conditions by regulations which "a century ago, or even half a century ago, probably would have been rejected as arbitrary and oppressive." . . . Clauses guaranteeing to the individual protection against specific abuses of power, must have a similar capacity of adaptation to a changing world. . . .

When the Fourth and Fifth Amendments were adopted, "the form that evil had theretofore taken," had been necessarily simple. Force and violence were then the only means known to man by which a Government could directly effect self-incrimination. It could compel the individual to testify—a compulsion effected, if need be, by torture. It could secure possession of his papers and other articles incident to his private life—a seizure effected, if need be, by breaking and entry. Protection against such invasion of "the sanctities of a man's home and the privacies of life" was provided in the Fourth and Fifth Amendments by specific language. . . . But "time works changes, brings into existence new conditions and purposes." Subtler and more far-reaching means of invading privacy have become available to the Government. Discovery and invention have made it possible for the Government, by means far more effective than stretching upon the rack, to obtain disclosure in court of what is whispered in the closet.

Moreover, "in the application of a constitution, our contemplation cannot be only of what has been but of what may be." The progress of science in furnishing the Government with means of espionage is not likely to stop with wire-tapping. Ways may some day be developed by which the Government, without removing papers from secret drawers, can reproduce them in court, and by which it will be enabled to expose to a jury the most intimate occurrences of the home. Advances in the psychic and related sciences may bring means of exploring unexpressed beliefs, thoughts and emotions. . . . Can it be that the Constitution affords no protection against such invasions of individual security?

A sufficient answer is found in *Boyd* v. *United States* . . . a case that will be remembered as long as civil liberty lives in the United States. This Court there reviewed the history that lay behind the Fourth and Fifth Amendments. We said with reference to Lord Camden's judgment in *Entick* v. *Carrington* . . . "The principles laid down in this opinion affect the very essence of constitutional liberty and security. They reach farther than the concrete form of the case there before the court, with its adventitious circumstances; they apply to all invasions on the part of the Government and its employees of the sanctities of a man's home and the privacies of life. It is not the breaking of his doors, and the rummaging of his drawers, that constitutes the essence of the offence; but it is the invasion of his indefeasible right of personal security, personal liberty and private property, where that right has never been forfeited by his conviction of some public offence,—it is the invasion of this sacred right which underlies and constitutes the essence of Lord Camden's judgment. Breaking into a house and opening boxes and drawers are circumstances of aggravation; but any forcible and compulsory extortion of a man's own testimony or of his private papers to be used as evidence of a crime or to forfeit his goods, is within the condemnation of that judgment. In this regard the Fourth and Fifth Amendments run almost into each other."

In *Ex parte Jackson* . . . it was held that a sealed letter entrusted to the mail is protected by the Amendments. The mail is a public service furnished by the Government. The telephone is a public service furnished by its authority. There is, in essence, no difference between the sealed letter and the private telephone message. As Judge Rudkin said below: "True the one is visible, the other invisible; the one is tangible, the other intangible; the one is sealed and the other unsealed, but these are distinctions without a difference." The evil incident to invasion of the privacy of the telephone is far greater than that involved in tampering with the mails. Whenever a telephone line is tapped, the privacy of the persons at both ends of the line is invaded and all conversations between them upon any subject, and although proper, confidential and privileged, may be overheard. Moreover, the tapping of one man's telephone line involves the tapping of the telephone of every other person whom he may call or who may call him. As a means of espionage, writs of assistance and general warrants are but puny instruments of tyranny and oppression when compared with wire-tapping.

Time and again, this Court, in giving effect to the principle underlying the Fourth Amendment, has refused to place an unduly literal construction upon it. This was notably illustrated in the *Boyd* case itself. Taking language in its ordinary meaning, there is no "search" or "seizure" when a defendant is required to produce a document in the orderly process of a court's procedure. "The right of the people to be secure in their persons, houses, papers, and effects, against unreasonable searches and seizures," would not be violated, under any ordinary construction of language, by compelling obedience to a subpoena. But this Court holds the evidence inadmissible simply because the information leading to the issue of the subpoena has been unlawfully secured. *Silverthorne Lumber Co.* v. *United States.* . . . Literally, there is no "search" or "seizure" when a friendly visitor abstracts papers from an office; yet we held in *Gouled* v. *United States* . . . that evidence so obtained could not be used. No court which looked at the words of the Amendment rather than at its underlying purpose would hold, as this Court did in *Ex parte Jackson,* that its protection extended to letters in the mails. The provision against self-incrimination in the Fifth Amendment has been given an equally broad construction. . . . The narrow language of the Amendment has been consistently construed in the light of its object, "to insure that a person should not be compelled, when acting as a witness in any investigation, to give testimony which might tend to show that he himself had committed a crime. The privilege is limited to criminal matters, but it is as broad as the mischief against which it seeks to guard."

Decisions of this Court applying the principle of the *Boyd* case have settled these things. Unjustified search and seizure violates the Fourth Amendment, whatever the character of the paper; whether the paper when taken by the federal officers was in the home, in an office or elsewhere; whether the taking was effected by force, by fraud, or in the orderly process of a court's procedure. From these decisions, it follows necessarily that the Amendment is violated by the officer's reading the paper without a physical seizure, without his even touching it; and that use, in any criminal proceeding, of the contents of the paper so examined—as where they are testified to by a federal officer who thus saw the document or where, through knowledge so obtained, a copy has been procured elsewhere—any such use constitutes a violation of the Fifth Amendment.

The protection guaranteed by the Amendments is much broader in scope. The makers of our Constitution undertook to secure conditions favorable to the pursuit of happiness. They recognized the significance of man's spiritual nature, of his feelings and of his intellect. They knew that only a part of the pain, pleasure and satisfactions of life are to be found in material things. They sought to protect Americans in their beliefs, their thoughts, their emotions and their sensations. They conferred, as against the Government, the right to be let alone—the most comprehensive of rights and the right most valued by civilized men. To protect that right, every unjustifiable intrusion by the Government upon the privacy of the individual, whatever the means employed, must be deemed a violation of the Fourth Amendment. And the use, as evidence in a criminal proceeding, of facts ascertained by such intrusion must be deemed a violation of the Fifth.

Applying to the Fourth and Fifth Amendments the established rule of construction, the defendants' objections to the evidence obtained by wire-tapping must, in my opinion, be sustained. It is, of course, immaterial where the physical connection with the telephone wires leading into the defendants' premises was made. And it is also immaterial that the intrusion was in aid of law enforcement. Experience should teach us to be most on our guard to protect liberty when the Government's purposes are beneficent. Men born to freedom are naturally alert to repel invasion of their liberty by evil-minded rulers. The greatest dangers to liberty lurk in insidious encroachment by men of zeal, well-meaning but without understanding.

Independently of the constitutional question, I am of opinion that the judgment should be reversed. By the laws of Washington, wire-tapping is a crime. . . . To prove its case, the Government was obliged to lay bare the crimes committed by its officers on its behalf. A federal court should not permit such a prosecution to continue. . . .

. . . The Eighteenth Amendment has not in terms empowered Congress to authorize anyone to violate the criminal laws of a State. And Congress has never purported to do so. . . . The terms of appointment of federal prohibition agents do not purport to confer upon them authority to violate any criminal law. Their superior officer, the Secretary of the Treasury, has not instructed them to commit crime on behalf of the United States. It may be assumed that the Attorney General of the United States did not give any such instruction.

When these unlawful acts were committed, they were crimes only of the officers individually. The Government was innocent, in legal contemplation; for no federal official is authorized to commit a crime on its behalf. When the Government, having full knowledge, sought, through the Department of Justice, to avail itself of the fruits of these acts in order to accomplish its own ends, it assumed moral responsibility for the officers' crimes. . . . And if this Court should permit the Government, by means of its officers' crimes, to effect its purpose of punishing the defendants, there would seem to be present all the elements of a ratification. If so, the Government itself would become a lawbreaker.

Will this Court by sustaining the judgment below sanction such conduct on the part of the Executive? The governing principle has long been settled. It is that a court will not redress a wrong when he who invokes its aid has unclean hands. The maxim of unclean hands comes from courts of equity. But the principle prevails also in courts of law. Its common application is in civil actions between private parties. Where the Government is the actor, the reasons for applying it are even more persuasive. Where the remedies invoked are those of the criminal law, the reasons are compelling. . . .

Decency, security and liberty alike demand that government officials shall be subjected to the same rules of conduct that are commands to the citizen. In a government of laws, existence of the government will be imperilled if it fails to observe the law scrupulously. Our Government is the potent, the omnipresent teacher. For good or for ill, it teaches the whole people by its example. Crime is contagious. If the Government becomes a lawbreaker, it breeds contempt for law; it invites every man to become a law unto himself; it invites anarchy. To declare that in the administration of the criminal law the end justifies the means—to declare that the Government may commit crimes in order to secure the conviction of a private criminal—would bring terrible retribution. Against that pernicious doctrine this Court should resolutely set its face.

MR. JUSTICE BUTLER, dissenting.

I sincerely regret that I cannot support the opinion and judgments of the Court in these cases.

The order allowing the writs of certiorari operated to limit arguments of counsel to the constitutional question. I do not participate in the controversy that has arisen here as to whether the evidence was inadmissible because the mode of obtaining it was unethical and a misdemeanor under state law. I prefer to say nothing concerning those questions because they are not within the jurisdiction taken by the order. . . .

The single question for consideration is this: May the Government, consistently with that clause [of the Fourth Amendment prohibiting "unreasonable searches and seizures"] have its officers whenever they see fit, tap wires, listen to, take down and report, the private messages and conversations transmitted by telephones? . . .

The question at issue depends upon a just appreciation of the facts.

Telephones are used generally for transmission of messages concerning official, social, business and personal affairs including communications that are private and privileged—those between physician and patient, lawyer and client, parent and child, husband and wife. The contracts between telephone companies and users contemplate the private use of the facilities employed in the service. The communications belong to the parties between whom they pass. During their transmission the exclusive use of the wire belongs to the persons served by it. Wire tapping involves interference with the wire while being used. Tapping the wires and listening in by the officers literally constituted a search for evidence. . . .

This Court has always construed the Constitution in the light of the principles upon which it was founded. The direct operation or literal meaning of the words used do not measure the purpose or scope of its provisions. Under the principles established and applied by this Court, the Fourth Amendment safeguards against all evils that are like and equivalent to those embraced within the ordinary meaning of its words. That construction is consonant with sound reason and in full accord with the course of decisions since *McCulloch* v. *Maryland*. That is the principle directly applied in the *Boyd* case.

When the facts in these cases are truly estimated, a

fair application of that principle decides the constitutional question in favor of the petitioners. With great deference, I think they should be given a new trial.

MR. JUSTICE STONE, dissenting.

I concur in the opinions of MR. JUSTICE HOLMES and MR. JUSTICE BRANDEIS. I agree also with that of MR. JUSTICE BUTLER so far as it deals with the merits. The effect of the order granting certiorari was to limit the argument to a single question, but I do not understand that it restrains the Court from a consideration of any question which we find to be presented by the record, for . . . this Court determines a case here on certiorari "with the same power and authority, and with like effect, as if the cause had been brought [here] by unrestricted writ of error or appeal."

CHAPTER

9

Impact

After the Supreme Court's opinion was announced, Roy Olmstead surrendered to federal authorities in Seattle and was returned to the penitentiary at McNeil Island to serve the remainder of his four-year term. As far as the judicial process was concerned, the Olmstead case was now closed; the convicted defendants had become problems for the officials who administered the federal penal system. Olmstead himself was a model prisoner, served his full sentence, and returned to Seattle, where he became a respected member of the community. Some years later he received a full pardon from the President. The mayor of Seattle was turned out of office at the next election.

The fate of Olmstead and the other principals in this case did nothing to solve two broader problems: bootlegging and wiretapping. The importation and sale of illegal liquor continued to grow, and the determination of most Americans to have legal abstinence along with their whiskey, gin, and beer made an increasing mockery of the Volstead Act and the Eighteenth Amendment. Indeed, while Olmstead had been on trial, prohibition agents were telling reporters of uncovering new liquor conspiracies along the West Coast that made Olmstead's gang look like a Sunday School class.

Repeal of the Eighteenth Amendment in 1933 ended prohibition as a federal issue but wiretapping has returned time and again to plague administrators, legislators, and judges. On the Supreme Court itself, rancor over the Olmstead case was slow in ebbing. A few days after the decision, Taft complained acidly to his brother that the minority had "abused us as encouragers of criminals in receiving the evidence of wiretapping as proper." The Chief noted that Brandeis had been "especially severe" in his criticism. "It is rather trying to have to be held up as immoral by one who is full of tricks all the time. But he can become full of eloquent denunciation without great effort. . . . His claques in the law school contingent will sound his praise and point the finger of scorn at us, but if they think we are going to be frightened in our effort to stand by the law and give the public a chance to punish criminals, they are mistaken, even though we are denounced for lack of high ideals." Stone and Holmes also came in for their full share of Taft's anger. Stone, he claimed, "has become entirely subservient to Holmes and Brandeis—I am very much disappointed in him." Holmes, dear old man that he was, had "little knowledge of governmental principles," and if his constitutional views ever were in the majority, "we should have no Constitution."[1]

A few days later Taft again unburdened himself to his brother. He said he had been deeply hurt by Holmes's dissent—"the nastiest opinion." More basically, the Chief felt a need to justify his decision:

> The telephone might just as well have been used to carry on a conspiracy to rob, to murder, to commit treason. The truth is we have to face the

> problems presented by new inventions. Many of them are most useful to criminals in their war against society and are at once availed of, and these idealist gentlemen urge a conclusion which facilitates crime by their use and furnishes immunity from conviction. . . . [2]

As is usual when the Court decides important cases, newspaper and magazine reaction to the *Olmstead* decision was divided, but the majority of editorials disapproved of what the Court had done. Eastern publications were particularly sharp in their comments. "Deplorable law and disgraceful ethics," *The Nation* observed caustically.[3] The *New York World* chided the justices for choosing "not to stand as a bulwark between this tyranny and the rights of the private citizen. . . ." The *New York Evening Post* charged that "The Supreme Court has been bewitched by prohibition." In an editorial entitled "Government Lawbreakers," The *New York Times* lamented: "Prohibition, having bred crimes innumerable, has succeeded in making Government the instigator, abettor and accomplice of crime. It has now made universal snooping possible."[4] The *Courier-Journal* of New Haven—the town where Taft had lived in the eight years between the White House and the Court, and which he had loved since his undergraduate days at Yale—was scathing in its criticism of his opinion:

> Instead of further protecting society from the criminal, the majority decision increases the possibility of criminal indulgence and of multiplying the number of criminals. Throwing the door wide open to the tapping of telephone wires by Tom, Dick, and Harry would seem to be a most dangerous contribution to the development of blackmail as well as straight crime.

The *Olmstead* decision had been announced on the last day of the 1927 term, and most of the justices had immediately left Washington. Taft would spend the summer at his lodge in Murray Bay, Canada; Brandeis would go to Cape Cod; Holmes to Beverly Farms, near Boston; the others would go to the Far West for hunting or fishing, or would join the tourists headed for Europe. Each would in his own way be seeking rest after the backbreaking work of disposing of over 850 cases in the previous eight months. The justices remained in contact with one another, however, and they could not help noticing newspaper reactions to the Olmstead case. Stone wrote Brandeis that he had been pleasantly surprised by the editorials. He had assumed the minority view would be unpopular, "but judging from nearly everything I have seen, and there is a great deal of it, sentiment in favor of individualism is not as dormant in this country as I had supposed."[5]

Taft viewed the editorials less happily. He had planned a visit to Yale and confessed to Van Devanter that he was now apprehensive about the trip, fearing that someone in New Haven might try to provoke him into a public debate. Van Devanter tried to reassure his old friend, but his report that Nicholas Murray Butler was shouted down at the Republican National Convention when he had tried to defend the *Olmstead* decision could hardly have comforted the Chief. Nor could Taft have drawn great solace from Van Devanter's reassurance that not all newspapers had been opposed—he had read a favorable editorial from Grand Rapids, Michigan. More soothing was Van Devanter's long-range view: "Time and experience will demonstrate that the decision is right, and it is better that the adverse comment that is made be not taken too seriously." Opposition, the justice flatly stated, came in large part from "the wets," who were against any decision that made enforcement of prohibition more effective. Opposition, Van Devanter continued, also came from another quarter: "Every communist in the country and every sympathizer with communism naturally will be against the decision, and so will those who call themselves reformers but are in truth infected with communism. We do not have to go far to see that this is so."[6]

During the summer months there were rumors of discontent among congressmen, as well as discussion of a new statute to outlaw wiretapping. Stone was delighted by this prospect, though he thought it unlikely to occur. He exclaimed to Brandeis: "What a wholesome thing it would be if that should come about."[7] Understandably, the majority of the justices made a different evaluation. Van Devanter, possibly worried about the Chief Justice's penchant for getting involved in legislative matters, especially when a proposal touched the power or dignity of the Court, wrote his friend:

> Personally I seriously doubt the propriety of making any concession in regard to the need for legislation. . . . To my mind there is no need for such legislation; nor is there any sound basis for making a legislative distinction in this regard between different classes of crimes. The agitation which followed the decision will gradually exhaust itself and the decision will come to be accepted as sound in principle and needed in practice.[8]

The justices could fume or chuckle at the reactions to the Olmstead case, but the next moves were up to the executive or legislative branches. The judiciary, or more precisely, one trial judge, two circuit judges, and five Supreme Court justices, had denied that wiretapping contravened the Constitution and had refused to forbid the use of evidence obtained by wiretapping in federal courts. The decision whether or not wiretapping would be widely used in federal criminal investigations was left to the executive and legislative branches.

As the *Brief for the United States* had indicated, wiretapping had been viewed in Washington, D.C., with mixed emotions. In fact, it was likely that the decision to use wiretapping against Olmstead had probably been a local one, since both the Justice Department and the Treasury Department officially disapproved of it. The question was now whether the Supreme Court's decision would bring about a change of mind and result in prohibition agents' and other federal officials' resorting to wiretapping on a large scale.

The answer of the prohibition service was clear. In December 1930, at a congressional hearing, Colonel Amos Woodcock, Director of the Bureau of Prohibition, engaged in the following colloquy with Representative Tinkham of Massachusetts:

Mr. TINKHAM: Is it your policy to permit the tapping of wires?

Mr. WOODCOCK: We do; and the Supreme Court has approved that practice.

Mr. TINKHAM: Do you approve of the practice of tapping wires?

Mr. WOODCOCK: I do. I have not qualms at all about that, sir. I think the telephone and telegraph franchises are given for the transaction of lawful business and the promotion of lawful commerce. I do not think that the unlawful have any right to use them with impunity. . . .

Mr. TINKHAM: Do you not think that the tapping of wires is a dirty practice, even in connecting [sic] with—

Mr. OLIVER [another member of the committee]: I think that is a matter of individual opinion.

Mr. TINKHAM: All right. Just one word. The minority

> of the Supreme Court called the tapping of wires dirty business and 27 States have made wire tapping a crime.[9]

The answer of the Bureau of Investigation was equally clear. As J. Edgar Hoover later privately assured Justice Stone, he was opposed to wiretapping as unethical conduct and insisted that BI agents observe Attorney General Stone's rule against wiretapping. In public Hoover was no less blunt in stating his position. At a congressional hearing in 1931, Representative Tinkham asked Hoover if any federal money was being spent for wiretapping. Hoover replied emphatically:

> No sir. We have a very definite rule in the bureau that any employee engaging in wiretapping will be dismissed from the service of the bureau. . . . While it may not be illegal, I think it is unethical, and it is not permitted under the regulations by the Attorney General.[10]

Hoover was giving no more than a fair summary of Section 14 of the rules of his bureau: "Wiretapping, entrapment, or use of any illegal or unethical tactics in procuring information will not be tolerated. . . ."

If prohibition enforcement had continued to be lodged in the Treasury Department, the conflict in policy would have been inconvenient but tolerable. In 1930, however, Congress transferred the Bureau of Prohibition to the Justice Department, and the conflict became less bearable. The following year, shortly after Hoover had publicly stated his opposition to wiretapping, William Mitchell, who had been promoted to Attorney General in 1929, stepped in. "The present condition in the Department cannot continue," he said. "We cannot have one bureau in which wiretapping is allowed and another in which it is prohibited. The same regulations must apply to all."[11] The Attorney General then issued an order authorizing BI and prohibition agents to wiretap, but only after securing the permission of their bureau chief as well as of the Assistant Attorney General in charge of the particular investigation. Prohibition agents used their power extensively, but Hoover continued to disapprove of the new dispensation and seldom authorized its employment.

Members of Congress were also concerned about wiretapping, but in the halcyon days of the 1920s life on Capitol Hill was more leisurely than it would soon become under the New Deal; and when the Olmstead case was decided Congress had already adjourned for the summer. In the short December–March session, with the stock market tumbling into what seemed to be a bottomless canyon—and many speculators following suit—wiretapping did not rate a high legislative priority. At the next session, however, congressional interest in this law-enforcement technique increased. A special committee to investigate wiretapping held an intensive inquiry, and Department of Justice officials were subjected to annual inquiries at appropriations hearings by congressmen who were against prohibition and/or were ardent civil libertarians. It was in response to such questions that Hoover and Woodcock had explained their views.

In early 1931 Representative Tinkham introduced an amendment to the Justice Department's appropriation bill forbidding the spending of money to finance wiretapping. To support his proposal, the congressman read into the record the testimony of Colonel Woodcock, comparing it with statements by J. Edgar Hoover. Despite the combined eloquence of Tinkham and Hoover, the amendment was defeated after a lively debate, 104–75.[12]

Tinkham and his friends had not given up, however. At the next hearings, Tinkham returned to the attack, this time against Attorney General Mitchell. Mitchell frankly conceded that wiretapping was easily susceptible of abuse, but pointed out that his order authorizing the tactic had the procedural safeguard of requiring approval by two responsible Justice Department officials. Later at the same hearing, the Attorney General explained that he thought it was irrelevant to any federal policy that many states had made wiretapping a crime. These statutes, he asserted, had not been intended to bar police tapping. More important, under the supremacy clause of Article VI of the Constitution, a state, even if it wanted to, could not legitimately interfere with a federal officer's carrying out his official duties.

Pressed by Tinkham to justify what the congressman asserted four justices had called a "more or less despicable" policy, Mitchell blandly replied that he was not aware that any of the justices had "talked about the policy of the thing being reprehensible or not." However, since the Court had held wiretapping did not violate the Constitution, the only question remaining was that of the most practical policy choice; and Mitchell claimed that the Department's regulations struck the best balance attainable between police efficiency and protection of individual rights. Bringing up an emotional argument which would be relied upon frequently by future attorneys general, Mitchell added:

> I feel sure that if that case of wiretapping . . . had been decided in a case where some young girl had been kidnapped, had been held for misuse or ransom, there would have been an overwhelming volume of approval by the people and the press of the country when the opinion was handed down.

> The disapproval that was expressed in some quarters I have always felt was affected very largely by people's attitude on prohibition.[13]

Ten months later Tinkham and Mitchell renewed their debate, and once again Mitchell repeated his opposition to both outlawing wiretapping and allowing it to exist without close safeguards.[14] Tinkham continued to press his attack, and if his debates with the Attorney General ended in a draw, at least in 1933 Congress did approve an amendment to the appropriation bill forbidding the Bureau of Prohibition—but not any other federal agency—to spend money to finance wiretapping.

As for the impact of the *Olmstead* decision on the lower courts, it seems generally to have been accepted. Chapter 1 pointed out that lower court judges often have considerable leeway in interpreting and applying the doctrines laid down by the Supreme Court. At least insofar as one can gather from the published decisions of lower federal courts—and not all of their decisions are published—federal trial judges made little deviation from the *Olmstead* rule. They allowed the government to introduce wiretap evidence where it chose to do so.

In permitting use of such evidence, the Olmstead case was simple, clear, and easy to follow. When, as we shall see, the Supreme Court in the late 1930s began to qualify the *Olmstead* rule by means of statutory interpretation, the justices thereby enlarged the area of lower court discretion; and federal judges were quick—indeed, they were forced—to offer solutions of their own to problems not specifically covered by the Court's new and more complex rules. Because of the divisions among the justices on wiretapping, district and circuit judges may well have seen themselves as faced with a choice between following the decision of yesterday or anticipating that of tomorrow. Under these circumstances, the attitude of federal judges toward *Olmstead* and its progeny is more accurately described as bureaucratic independence than as bureaucratic resistance. *Olmstead,* of course, settled only that wiretapping did not violate the federal Constitution; the judges of each state were left free to decide whether state laws and constitutional provisions forbade or permitted such practices.

With the coming of the New Deal and the end of prohibition, wiretapping for a time lost its prominence as a public policy issue. Federal officials on a small scale and state police and private detectives in increasingly large numbers went blithely about the business of eavesdropping on telephone conversations. The only hint of congressional action came in the Federal Communications Act of 1934. Section 605 of this statute provided in part:

> no person not being authorized by the sender shall intercept any communication and divulge or publish the existence, contents, substance, purport, effect or meaning of such intercepted communication to any person. . . .

Section 501 of the Act made wilful violation punishable by fine and imprisonment.

However pertinent to wiretapping Section 605 seems in retrospect, it must be kept in mind that this statute had been pushed through Congress as basically no more than a revision and recodification of existing federal regulations governing radio broadcasting. No mention of wiretapping had been made in the committee hearings, in the committee reports, or in debate in either house of Congress. A few years later, when a man who had been convicted in a federal court on the basis of wiretapping evidence raised the point that Section 605 made wiretapping a federal crime and thereby rendered such evidence inadmissible, the trial judge and a unanimous Circuit Court of Appeals summarily dismissed his claim.[15]

When this case, *Nardone* v. *United States*,[16] reached the Supreme Court in 1937, the justices burst the bubble of legality that had protected the Justice Department's policy. Only five of the justices who had sat on the Olmstead case were still on the Court and only two, Sutherland and McReynolds, were from the old majority. These two stood firm. But Brandeis, Butler, and Stone joined with four new members of the Court, Charles Evans Hughes, Owen J. Roberts, Benjamin N. Cardozo, and Hugo L. Black, to rule that in Section 605 Congress had forbidden wiretapping without the consent of the sender of the message, and therefore such evidence, since secured in violation of an act of Congress, could not be used in a federal court.

Nardone was retried and convicted again. Once more he obtained Supreme Court review of his case. This time the justices held not only that direct wiretap evidence was inadmissible but also that evidence which had been obtained through leads secured by wiretapping was similarly barred.[17] Apparently unwilling to give up, the Justice Department brought several more wiretapping cases. If these cases represented attempts to probe for loopholes in the Nardone rulings, their mission was a failure. The Supreme Court and Circuit Courts of Appeals stuck firmly to the letter and spirit of the Nardone decisions: wiretapping was a federal crime.[18] *Olmstead*, however, had not been overruled. The Nardone cases had been based solely on statutory interpretation. Essentially they said no more than that Congress had imposed on federal officers even tighter restrictions than had the Constitution. A decision that Congress has chosen not to exercise the full authority granted by the Constitution does not, of course, reverse a previous decision that the power in question can be exercised consistent with the Constitution. While not overruling *Olmstead*, the Nardone cases obviously and effectively undermined the practical value of *Olmstead* as a precedent—at least, so long as Congress did not amend the Federal Communications Act.

After the Nardone rulings the proponents of wiretapping directed their activities toward Capitol Hill and tried to secure just such an amendment. Their big chance came in 1938 after the first Nardone ruling, when each house passed its own version of a bill to permit wiretapping by federal agents with the approval of their department chiefs. The two bills, however, were somewhat different in form, and both failed to become law when their differences were not compromised prior to adjournment.

The next year another proposal to amend Section 605 was before Congress, but by this time the old divisions within the executive department had again begun to manifest themselves. J. Edgar Hoover, in a letter later made public, advised the Attorney General: "While I concede that the telephone tap is from time to time of limited value in the criminal investigative field, I frankly and sincerely believe that if a statute of this kind were enacted the abuses arising therefrom would far outweigh the value which might accrue to law enforcement as a whole."[19] In 1940 a Senate committee put forth similar sentiments, branding wiretapping as especially dangerous in that its use threatened to set up a government spy system.[20]

In March 1940, shortly after the publication of the report of the Senate committee, Attorney General Robert H. Jackson issued a new directive reinstating as Justice Department policy the pre-1931 rule of the FBI banning wiretapping. As head of the Justice Department, Jackson had no authority over the investigation of offenses under the narcotics, tax, and mail statutes, but he could control United States Attorneys, who would have to prosecute such crimes; and Jackson's order forbade these officials to initiate, after April 1, 1940, prosecution of any case in which wiretap evidence had been used, at least not without a specific order from the Attorney General.[21]

Justice Department practice, however, did not conform to this rigid line. On May 21, 1940, two months after the publication of Jackson's order, President Roosevelt sent the Attorney General a hastily composed letter stating that he was "convinced" the Supreme Court had never meant to imply that wiretapping was illegal where national security was involved. He added:

> You are, therefore, authorized and directed, in such cases as you may approve, after investigation of the need in each case, to authorize the necessary investigating agents that they are at liberty to secure information by listening devices directed to the conversations or other communications of persons suspected of subversive activities against the Government of the United States, including suspected spies. You are requested furthermore to limit these investigations so conducted to a minimum and to limit them in so far as possible to aliens.[22]

With the United States about to be embroiled in World War II, the number of persons suspected of engaging in subversive activities would increase to large proportions.

Meanwhile Jackson again asked Congress to change the law to allow wiretapping in a limited number of situations. In 1940 one bill was favorably reported by the House Judiciary Committee, but legislators took no further action at that session. The following year a fresh batch of proposals was introduced, and the hearings conducted by the House Judiciary Committee brought out once more the division of sentiment within the Executive Department. The bill receiving the most serious attention was that of Representative Hobbs of Alabama. It would have allowed federal officers, with the consent of their agency head, to tap telephones to aid in the investigation of any felony. Jackson endorsed Hobbs's proposal, though he added diplomatically that he would have no objection to restricting the authorization to crimes involving espionage, sabotage, kidnapping, extortion, and violations of narcotics laws.[23]

In his endorsement, the Attorney General admitted that at least in one kidnapping case he had, contrary to his own 1940 policy, ordered Hoover to install a telephone tap. More important than this admission was a startlingly new interpretation Jackson offered of Section 605:

> There is no Federal statute that prohibits or punishes wire tapping alone. The only offense under the present law is to intercept any communication and divulge or publish the same. . . . To use evidence obtained by wire tapping for the protection of society against criminals often requires that it be divulged in open court. It is this divulging [rather than the tapping itself] in law enforcement that court decisions hold to violate the statute.[24]

J. Edgar Hoover's views were also put before the committee. He said he could endorse the bill only if it were limited to the kinds of crimes the Attorney General had mentioned. Interestingly, Hoover's position had now changed from blanket disapproval of wiretapping to disapproval only of "uncontrolled and unrestrained wire tapping by law-enforcement officials." Under strict supervision, and where serious crimes were involved, the FBI Chief stated, wiretapping "as an investigative function is of considerable importance." Hoover gave a hint of the reasons behind his shift: "I also feel that world developments of the past year or more, and the changed conditions resulting therefrom, have increased the gravity from the standpoint of national safety of such offenses as espionage and sabotage."[25]

Another executive official managed to get his opinion on the public record. In reply to an inquiry from Congressman Thomas Eliot, Franklin D. Roosevelt wrote a long letter explaining his reaction to Hobbs's bill. Usually such correspondence is carefully prearranged, and the letter from the President is drafted by the head of the executive agency most immediately concerned—in this instance the Department of Justice. But the tone of Roosevelt's letter and its subtle differences of outlook from those of both Jackson and Hoover indicate that the President had given some personal attention and thought to his answer.

Roosevelt began by noting that he had read the bill and had "no hesitation in saying that it goes entirely too far and that its provisions are unnecessarily broad." The President continued:

> It is more than desirable, it is necessary that criminals be detected and prosecuted vigilantly as possible. It is more necessary that the citizens of a democracy be protected in their rights of privacy from unwarranted snooping. As an instrument for oppression of free citizens, I can think of none worse than indiscriminate wiretapping. . . . In general, my own personal point of view is close to that of Justice Holmes in his famous dissent in the *Olmstead* case, when he said: "We have to choose, and for my part I think it a less evil that some criminals should escape than that the Government should play an ignoble part."[26]

On the other hand, Roosevelt conceded that the telephone was a particularly valuable instrument to criminals engaged in offenses against national security or in kidnapping and extortion. He suggested, therefore, that a satisfactory bill should limit wiretapping to those classes of crimes, restrict authority to the Department of Justice alone, and require an order personally signed by the Attorney General before officials could tap a telephone.

In October 1941, with no new legislation yet enacted, Francis Biddle, who had become Attorney General when Robert H. Jackson was appointed to the Supreme Court, announced a new policy. Following Jackson's earlier interpretation of the law, Biddle asserted that Section 605 forbade tapping *plus* disclosure, not merely wiretapping. And, in his opinion, mere reporting by a government agent to his superior of what he had overheard on a wiretap did not constitute disclosure. On the basis of this reasoning, Biddle established a policy—one apparently followed by his successors to date—allowing FBI agents to tap wires in cases involving national security or in serious crimes such as kidnapping. But FBI agents must first secure the permission of the Director of the FBI and of the Attorney General himself.[27] For obvious reasons, this policy was much the same as that the President had outlined in his letter to Representative Eliot.

CHAPTER

10

Olmstead Revisited

The Nardone cases had put *Olmstead* v. *United States* in a state of legal limbo. Neither Nardone decision had overruled *Olmstead*, but insofar as federal courts were concerned—and perhaps even state tribunals, though this was still uncertain—wiretapping evidence after 1938 was inadmissible. Indeed, the second Nardone case made it very possible that use of wiretapping in an investigation might make inadmissible much of the prosecution's evidence not directly obtained through eavesdropping techniques.

Congressional failure to respond fully to the somewhat uncertain requests of administration officials for amendments to Section 605 did nothing to breathe new life into *Olmstead*. Since Attorney General Jackson's order ending wiretapping had not gone into effect until the spring of 1940 and since investigation and prosecution of a serious crime normally take years to reach the Supreme Court, it was not improbable to foresee, in the early 1940s, that the *Olmstead* battle would be refought. And given the apparent sensitivity to civil liberties claims of the younger justices whom Roosevelt had appointed to the Court, it was open to question whether another five-justice majority could be mustered to approve the constitutionality of wiretapping.

The occasion for battle was soon before the justices in the case of *Goldman* v. *United States*,[1] though the issue would be cloaked in a more difficult form than *Olmstead* had presented. In January 1940, before Jackson's ban on telephone tapping, the U.S. Attorney in New York City had secured an indictment against three lawyers for conspiring to violate the bankruptcy act. Evidence against the defendants had been obtained in part through eavesdropping which had involved listening in on telephone conversations, though without directly tapping into the lines themselves.

Federal agents, with the cooperation of the building superintendent, had entered the office of one of the defendants and installed a listening device. The device failed to function properly; but the agents, who occupied the adjacent office, utilized a detectaphone—an instrument which can amplify the sound of voices talking on the other side of a wall—and transcribed a number of incriminating conversations, including several made during telephone calls.

The defendants were convicted and their convictions upheld by the Circuit Court of Appeals for the Second Circuit. The Supreme Court granted certiorari, and *Goldman* v. *United States* was first argued in the 1940 term. In June 1941, the justices requested that counsel reargue the case during the following term.

By the 1941 term, Harlan Stone was Chief Justice, the only member of the Court who had sat on the Olmstead case. Stone, it will be recalled, had been one of the dissenters. Owen J. Roberts, the senior associate justice, had come to the Court in 1930, after Justice Sanford's death. The other seven justices had all been appointed by Franklin D. Roosevelt. Stanley Reed of Kentucky and James Byrnes of South Carolina were regarded as relatively conservative; they were not considered civil libertarians. Hugo Black, Felix Frankfurter, William Douglas, Frank Murphy, and Robert Jackson were known, in varying degrees, as avid defenders of civil liberties. Their attitude toward wiretapping was curiously ambivalent, however. As Attorney General, Murphy had permitted wiretapping, even after the Nardone decisions. Yet once on the bench, he looked with horror on wiretapping, just as he did on several Department of Justice policies he had approved when in the executive branch.

Jackson's involvement in the wiretapping controversy has already been recounted, and he would not take part in the Goldman litigation. He felt that since the indictment had been brought when he was Attorney General, he should not participate. Justice Murphy, who had been in charge of the Department of Justice when the *Goldman* investigation had been conducted, felt no such compunction. Actually, the decision of a justice not to participate in a case is a personal one. Each justice decides it according to the dictates of his own conscience, and Murphy's participation was no reflection on his honor. After all, the Olmstead case had been argued by two of Pierce Butler's former law partners and the indictment had been obtained when Stone was Attorney General. Both justices had taken part in that case. It is a rare occasion when an Attorney General has any real part in—or even information about—a small-scale prosecution brought by a U.S. Attorney. Probably neither Murphy nor Jackson had any knowledge about the activities of federal agents in the Goldman case, though both had been formally responsible for the policies of the Justice Department regarding wiretapping.

Justice Frankfurter had made no bones about his strong personal disapproval of wiretapping, and he had written the opinion of the Court in the second Nardone case. But that decision had been based on statutory interpretation and rules of evidence, not on constitutional grounds; and Frankfurter's reputation as a civil libertarian was qualified by a reluctance to find legislative or executive action unconstitutional. As a critic of the Court during the 1920s and 1930s, he had sharply taken to task the old justices for reading their own predilections into the Constitution, and since coming to the bench Frankfurter had always been quick to distinguish between what he said were his personal preferences and what he identified as the commands of the Constitution. In procedural matters or in those of statutory interpretation, he normally took the course that least restricted individual rights. In constitutional cases, however, he typically upheld the decisions of other federal officials.

Black and Douglas were usually even more sensitive to civil liberties claims than Frankfurter, and they did not share his deep reluctance to base decisions on constitutional grounds. But in the 1940s these two justices had a peculiar blind spot: neither of them showed particular concern about the right of privacy. In later years, both justices, Douglas more so than Black, would become more responsive to privacy claims. In 1942, however, their views on the Fourth Amendment had not yet crystallized into the strong activism they would later display.

The Goldman case was discussed at conference in early February 1942. Justice Murphy's notes on that conference,[2] while not complete, are fairly detailed and indicate that the discussion was lively and heated. Chief Justice Stone began by summing up the facts of the case. The central problem, the Chief Justice said, was *Olmstead*. Read carefully, that case could be distinguished from *Goldman*, but he thought the Court had to consider whether it should be overruled. The Fourth Amendment, Stone admitted, was not very specific about how far privacy should be protected. Some invasions of privacy, such as eavesdropping without trespassing, had historically been allowed by American judges. The vice of the sort of eavesdropping in this case, he thought, was that it was totally unrestrained. Federal agents had not sought a search warrant; in fact, unless they already had had considerable evidence linking the defendants to a crime, it was unlikely that they would have been able to show the probable cause necessary to obtain a warrant. Stone concluded on the note that while he did not think the case was "dead open and shut," he leaned toward reversing the convictions.

Roberts and Reed took a strong position to affirm. Roberts candidly stated that he did not believe the Fourth Amendment had been intended to prevent police snooping, and Reed felt that the situation was completely covered by *Olmstead* v. *United States.* Black, Douglas, and Byrnes merely noted their votes to affirm the convictions. Frankfurter attacked both Roberts' interpretation of the Constitution and Reed's faith in *Olmstead* as a precedent to be followed. He then stated at some length his own revulsion at wiretapping as an invasion of the right to privacy.

When the discussion had played itself out, Stone called for a vote. The Court was five to affirm the convictions—Roberts, Black, Reed, Douglas, and Byrnes—and three to reverse—Stone, Frankfurter, and Murphy.

As the senior majority justice, Roberts assigned himself the task of writing the opinion. He held that use of the detectaphone did not violate the Federal Communications Act, nor, under the doctrine of *Olmstead,* did it contravene the Fourth Amendment. He also stated that whatever trespass the agents had committed in installing the unsuccessful listening device did not make inadmissible any evidence later obtained through the detectaphone. For the dissenters Stone undertook to write an opinion, and Murphy gave general directions to guide his clerk in preparing a second dissent.[3]

Stone quickly drafted his opinion; by February 27, he had incorporated some minor suggestions by Frankfurter. At this point the draft read:

> Had a majority of the Court been willing at this time to overrule the *Olmstead* case, we would have been happy to join them. But as they have declined to do so, and as we think this case is indistinguishable in principle from *Olmstead's*, we have no occasion to repeat here the dissenting views in that case with which we agree.
>
> Both courts below found that the trespass by the Government officers in locating the dictaphone did not aid materially in the use of the detectaphone. Hence it is unnecessary to consider whether the use of the detectaphone, if aided by the trespass, would constitute a violation of the Fourth Amendment. The Government did not deny that it would, and we explicitly dissociate ourselves from the declaration in the opinion [of the Court] that it would not.[4]

When Roberts read the second paragraph of Stone's opinion, he agreed to modify what he had said about the trespass and substantially adopted Stone's phrasing: "Both courts below have found that the trespass did not aid materially in the use of the detectaphone. Since we accept these concurrent findings, we need not consider a contention based on a denial of their verity." Having achieved this minor victory, Stone dropped the second paragraph of his opinion.

Meanwhile, when the Chief Justice's opinion came to Murphy's office, his law clerk sent it on to the Justice with a report that he had just had a visit from one of Stone's clerks who said that Frankfurter was champing at the bit to write a searing dissent. The Chief Justice, however, was convinced that it was wiser for the minority to take a beating now without putting up a public fight on *Olmstead*, lest that case become even more entrenched as the survivor of two great battles within the Court. Murphy's clerk added as a countervailing consideration that it might also be true that Brandeis' arguments in favor of privacy should be repeated every so often.

Murphy may have remembered that at the conference Stone had suggested that *Olmstead* might be overruled, but had not pressed the point; in fact, he had also suggested that it could be distinguished. Moreover, the Chief Justice had admitted that historically many different kinds of invasions of privacy had been allowed under the Fourth Amendment. Perhaps because of this recollection Murphy was unsure that Stone was fully committed to overturning *Olmstead*. In any event, he continued work on his own dissent. On March 5 Frankfurter, who by now had been won over to Stone's strategy of avoiding open conflict, tried to dissuade Murphy:

> You have heard my views expressed in Conference, and I am afraid somewhat fiercely, on wiretapping, and you must, therefore, know that I am as uncompromising on that subject as you are, feeling as you do that the issue goes to the very essence of a civilized society. Like you, therefore, I will not yield an inch on my convictions and would accede to no compromising expression of them.
>
> But I do not see that any "compromise" is involved in the way in which the C. J. has formulated dissent from the majority opinion. Of course each man's phrasing has its own distinctive quality,

> but so far as the substance of the matter goes, I certainly could not dream of improving on what Brandeis and Holmes said in the *Olmstead* case. And so it seems to me that an unequivocal announcement that we would overrule the *Olmstead* case and adopt as our own the views expressed by the dissenters in that case, is an unswerving and unqualified adoption of those views and a reaffirmation of them. And to do it in the way in which the Chief Justice proposes has for me the quality of Doric eloquence. Simplicity and austerity are sometimes the most emphatic way of conveying an idea to the world.[5]

In closing his letter, Frankfurter added a plea for solidarity:

> For the three of us to speak in different language would imply a difference of opinion amongst us. That would attenuate the moral strength of our position. I hope very much, therefore, that it will commend itself to you to have the three of us speak with one voice and in the way in which the C. J. has proposed.

Murphy, however, stuck to his own plan and circulated a long and eloquent dissent, asserting that government officers had committed a palpable invasion of defendants' privacy in violation of explicit prohibitions of the Fourth Amendment. In his opinion he referred to the federal agents as "over-zealous officials," and castigated their action as "debasing to government." When he received his copy, Frankfurter made only a few small suggestions and concluded: "You have not only expressed your convictions but you have expressed them, if I may say so, well."[6]

When Murphy's dissent was circulated to the full

Court, Justice Jackson was so stung by the derogatory comments about federal officials that he drafted an opinion of his own explaining why he was not participating and stating that the eavesdropping had been carried on under regulations approved by his predecessor as Attorney General—who, as everyone knew, was Frank Murphy. Murphy quickly saw that Jackson had him at a serious disadvantage and agreed to delete the objectionable phrases. Jackson, in turn, withdrew his separate opinion.

The refusal of the majority in *Goldman* to reverse *Olmstead* did not clarify the problems raised by the wiretapping policies laid down by Attorneys General Jackson and Biddle, but at least *Goldman* provided a crutch to stabilize federal practice. State officials were in a more confused situation than were federal officers. No case involving wiretapping by state or local police reached the Supreme Court until 1952, and it was not until *Wolf* v. *Colorado*,[7] decided in 1949, that the justices gave a clear indication of the law they would apply. The Wolf case was a review of a state conviction of an abortionist, a conviction based in part on evidence that local police had obtained through an illegal search and seizure of the defendant's office. For a majority of the Court, Justice Frankfurter held that the Fourteenth Amendment had made the Fourth Amendment equally binding on the states as on the federal government. But Frankfurter also declared that the *Weeks* rule excluding unconstitutionally obtained evidence—and, by implication, the *Nardone* rule excluding evidence secured in violation of a federal statute—was only a matter of practice in federal courts, not a principle of constitutional law. States were, therefore, free to use or not to use such contaminated evidence, though the officers who obtained it violated the Constitution and perhaps a federal statute as well.

In 1952, the Court in *Schwartz* v. *Texas*[8] made explicit what had been implicit in *Wolf*. Schwartz had been convicted in a state court on a robbery charge, and some of the evidence against him had been obtained through wiretapping. Texas courts sustained the admission of such evidence, and the U.S. Supreme Court granted certiorari to answer the question whether Section 605 forbade use of such evidence in a state court. Speaking for himself and five other justices, Sherman Minton wrote an opinion affirming the conviction. Minton leaned heavily on *Wolf* and held that states were free to follow the old common law practice of admitting evidence regardless of the method employed to secure it.*

Justice Black noted simply that he concurred in the result. Frankfurter and Douglas faced more difficult problems. Frankfurter still thought wiretapping unconstitutional, but he had also been the author of the Court's opinion in the Wolf case. Torn between two values, he wrote a short concurring opinion explaining his peculiar position and why he joined in the majority decision. Douglas, who had voted with the majority in *Goldman*, now confessed that he had been wrong. He had come to believe that wiretapping was unconstitutional and should not be admitted in either state or federal courts.

Schwartz may have clarified the law, but it did so at the price of muddling practice. As a leading authority on wiretapping has observed:

> State law as to wiretapping in 1952 was outwardly restrictive but was almost wholly ineffectual. Only one state (New York) supervised police wiretapping by court order; several states, such as

* Despite the broadness of this and other pronouncements, the Supreme Court has not allowed states to use evidence obtained through physical or psychological coercion.

> Louisiana, gave police the right to tap wires on their own authority; thirty-eight states had statutes generally forbidding any person to intercept telephone or telegraph messages. However, none of these thirty-eight statutes specifically mentioned police officers as persons forbidden to tap telephones, and no state before 1952 had interpreted its law to forbid police interceptions. In addition, more than half of the states in 1952 allowed evidence obtained illegally—including wiretap evidence—to be used in criminal trials.[9]

New York experience did not indicate that judicial supervision could be very close. In New York City alone, police in 1953–54 were tapping over 3500 telephones, almost half of them public phone booths, open to anyone with one dime or two nickels. In 1957, the Supreme Court in *Benanti* v. *United States*[10] cleared up any doubt about the criminal nature of such operations by ruling that state officials violated Section 605 in tapping telephones, and such evidence could no more be used in a federal court than if federal officers had installed the taps. Despite the Benanti decision and candid admissions from many state officials that they have been running taps as a standard method of investigation, the Department of Justice as of January 1965 had not yet secured an indictment against a policeman for violating Section 605 in the line of duty.

Private investigators have been far less discriminating than police in their use of wiretapping. The wiretap, whether done in the old-fashioned way or through more modern devices which permit eavesdropping without actually cutting into a power line, has opened a wide and lucrative field for unscrupulous private investigators who seek information for clients or for blackmail. Testifying before a California legislative committee in 1957, a well-known "sound engineer" explained at length how he sold his services to owners of department stores and hotels and on one occasion had even "bugged" a casket with a tape recorder.[11]

Nor is wiretapping the most efficient kind of eavesdropping. In *On Lee* v. *United States*[12] the Supreme Court by a five to four vote sustained a conviction based on evidence obtained through a radioed conversation between a special federal agent and the defendant. On two separate occasions the special agent, of unsavory background himself, had talked to the defendant about buying narcotics, and in the course of these conversations the defendant had made damaging admissions. Unknown to the defendant, the special agent had been carrying a microphone and transmitter, and both conversations had been broadcast to narcotics officials.

The detectaphone used in the Goldman case made it possible to hear entire conversations in offices or apartments, but posed serious problems in eavesdropping on conversations in private homes. The advent of the transistor has meant that this practical problem can frequently be overcome. Transistor-powered radio broadcasters can be made almost paper thin and can easily be hidden in a house to monitor all noises. These transmitters have the further advantage of not having a wire that can be used to trace the eavesdropper to his criminal act.*

* Today, to avoid having a man constantly in attendance at an eavesdropping post, as well as to overcome the sort of problems federal agents experienced in transcribing evidence from the Olmstead conversations, it has become standard technique to attach listening devices to a tape recorder. At first glance this method appears only to substitute total recall for fallible memory and possibly incoherent notes. The rub comes in the fact that a "sound engineer" can readily edit a tape. By breaking up individual syllables and sounds made by a speaker in the course of a conversation, a skillful engineer can put these sounds back together into any order he—or his employer—wishes. Since the

One of the most shocking cases involving this sort of electronic eavesdropping came to the Supreme Court in *Irvine* v. *California*.[13] Los Angeles police, accompanied by a professional "sound engineer," used a skeleton key to enter the home of a suspected bookmaker and planted a microphone in a closet. (The device was an old-fashioned one, equipped with a wire rather than a transistor transmitter.) When this arrangement proved acoustically unsound, the police and the engineer returned to the suspect's home and moved the mike to the bedroom the suspect shared with his wife. Shortly thereafter, the engineer had to go back a third time and eliminate a "hum" from the line. Finally, when properly installed, the mike was sufficiently sensitive to pick up both sides of telephone conversations, if each party spoke loudly and clearly.

With the evidence thus obtained, the district attorney had no difficulty in getting a conviction. Despite the fact that police had been guilty of breaking and entering as well as of trespassing and possibly of burglary, California courts admitted the evidence. When the case reached the U.S. Supreme Court, some of the justices expressed amazement and disgust at these crass invasions of privacy. Six of the justices, however, were of the opinion that *Wolf* v. *Colorado* was still controlling, and therefore the *Weeks* rule could not be forced on an unwilling state. Two members of the majority expressed a strong desire that the Justice Department prosecute the persons involved in the investigation, but federal officials decided against such a move.

---

inflection and pronunciation remain those of the speaker, it is virtually impossible to tell when a tape recording is a true record. See especially the testimony of Samuel Dash, U.S. Congress, Senate, Subcommittee on Constitutional Rights, *Wiretapping and Eavesdropping: Hearings*, 87th Cong., 1st Sess., pp. 118–19 (1961).

In recent years, more and more states have been enacting statutes prohibiting or restricting wiretapping by private citizens and/or public officials. Maryland, Nevada, and Oregon, for instance, have tightened controls over police by adopting legislation similar to that of New York, requiring a court order to install a wiretap. Pennsylvania and Illinois have outlawed all wiretaps, and Texas has made wiretap evidence inadmissible in state courts. Federal prosecutions under Section 605 have also increased, though the twelve prosecutions and ten convictions for 605 violations during the period from 1954 to 1961 probably did not frighten many eavesdroppers, especially since none of the accused was a government official.

Since Attorney General Biddle's order in 1941, federal practice has continued much the same under each succeeding Attorney General. Wiretapping has been used in investigations involving national security or in serious offenses such as kidnapping. From time to time J. Edgar Hoover or an Attorney General has made public an approximate count of the number of operating wiretaps run by the FBI; but about the only time the U.S. Attorneys have tried to use such evidence in court has been when officers have eavesdropped on a telephone line—as in solving the Sinatra kidnapping—with the permission of a person expecting to receive a call in an extortion case. In spite of the fact that Section 605 stipulates that the contents of an intercepted telephonic conversation may not be divulged without the consent of the "sender," the Supreme Court has held that the permission of the receiver is sufficient to allow evidence so obtained to be used in a federal court.[14]

In 1950 the espionage trial of Judith Coplon revealed the extent to which the FBI would go in tapping telephone lines. Some fifty agents had maintained 'round-the-clock surveillance of her home and office telephones and those of her family and her alleged Russian lover to whom she was accused of passing government secrets. These taps were continued during the pretrial stage of the legal proceedings, and the conversations monitored included some between Miss Coplon and her lawyer in which they discussed defense strategy at the trial. This flagrant violation of the historic right of confidential communication between an attorney and client brought about a reversal of Miss Coplon's conviction.[15]

As the Coplon case indicated, the Justice Department's interpretation of Section 605 gives the FBI considerable leeway in wiretapping. When the defense is able, as was Miss Coplon's lawyer, to expose the use of taps, a federal trial judge will quash the evidence so obtained or an appellate court will reverse the conviction. When a defense attorney cannot show that wiretapping has been used against his client, Justice Department officials apparently feel under no obligation to apprise courts of their use of wiretapping. Under such circumstances, there is little federal judges can do to protect a defendant's right to privacy.

From the Goldman decision until 1949, when the first comprehensive federal loyalty-security program since the Civil War was getting into high gear, the Department of Justice did not again press Congress to modify Section 605. In 1949 the Department asked for new legislation, but almost immediately withdrew its request. In recent years, however, the appearance of the Attorney General, whether a Democrat or a Republican, before a congressional committee to ask for a change in the law has become an almost annual occurrence. Although Senate and House committees have held a number of hearings, and occasionally the House has approved a bill, as of June 1965 no proposal to legalize wiretapping or to permit the use in evidence of information so obtained had successfully run the legislative gauntlet.

The Olmstead and Nardone cases continue to be ruling law, although the orders of the Attorney General still frame federal practice. The opinion in *Schwartz* v. *Texas*, although as the next chapter will indicate its authority has been weakened, coupled with the Department of Justice refusal to prosecute police for violating Section 605, allows each state to set its own policy on wiretapping.

CHAPTER

11

Conclusion

The zealous efforts of prohibition agents to dry up Seattle's supply of alcoholic beverages bore far greater fruit than any of the principals in the Olmstead case could have foreseen. The point of the Olmstead case is not that a small group of federal agents in Seattle caused the problem, but that their work provided an occasion that would be seized by judges, by administrators, and, to a lesser extent, by legislators to try to resolve the question of wiretapping.

Olmstead and its progeny illustrate the old truism that the justices of the Supreme Court help make law and, thereby, public policy. Despite their broad vision, the framers of the Constitution and the Bill of Rights had not foreseen electronic surveillance. In the cases before them, the justices had to repair this oversight by applying their own notions of the judicial function as well as of the good life.

These cases and the practices that preceded, followed, and accompanied them demonstrate with equal force that judges play only one part in formulating public policy. Orders of the President, the Attorney General, and the Director of the FBI, decisions of U.S. Attorneys not to prosecute local police for violations of Section 605, and the action and inaction of members of Congress have had as much to do as court decisions with whether or not wiretapping will be used as a standard technique in criminal investigations.

What has emerged from this interaction among judicial, executive, and legislative officials and private citizens is a series of policies, not one policy; and existing policies are not likely to be any more permanent than previous ones have been. The likelihood of change is increased by the number of government officials, state and federal, who share in the task of shaping public policy in the United States.

One of the more interesting aspects of the wiretapping problem has been the relative inactivity of Congress, the branch of government one usually associates most closely with the formulation of broad public policy in domestic affairs. Except for the restrictive rider on the appropriation bill passed in 1933 and Section 605 of the Federal Communications Act of 1934 (and it will be recalled that there is considerable doubt whether many members of Congress intended or understood Section 605 to outlaw telephone taps), the dozens of hearings conducted by various House and Senate committees since *Olmstead* have yielded no legislation other than a minor amendment changing the penalties for illegal wiretapping. As on so many other policy issues, Congress has been locked on dead center. Some federal executive officials, police associations, and conservative groups have prodded congressmen to repeal or materially modify Section 605, as have genuine fears of increased activities by criminal syndicates and espionage operations by foreign agents.

On the other hand, members of Congress have also been aware, or have been made aware by civil liberties organizations and some federal officials, of the dangers of wiretapping—its boundless potential for blackmail and police invasions of the privacy of the home. Words, like ideas, can be effective political weapons, and the eloquent dissents of Justices Holmes and Brandeis in *Olmstead* have been powerful instruments in the hands of civil libertarians. In particular, Holmes's phrase "dirty business" has kept the defenders of wiretapping at a moral disadvantage for almost forty years, the more so because time and again eavesdroppers have brought scandal upon themselves and their employers. The prospect of leading party politicians' listening in on each other's telephone calls, as actually happened in California in 1939–40, is hardly pleasant, though it is less shocking than the charges made in 1940 that some federal officers had authorized the tapping of Supreme Court telephones in order to find out how a pending case would be decided. Carefully documented instances, such as the Irvine and Coplon cases, of callous disregard by some police officials of constitutional rights do little to build congressional faith that increased authority to use wiretapping will not be abused.

Subjected to these pulls and counterpulls and finding a general state of public apathy about the wiretapping problem, most congressmen have to date opted for inaction. This choice has been made easier by the fact that permissive Justice Department policies toward wiretapping by federal and state officers have made it impossible for police to demonstrate a crisis in law enforcement which would be remedied by substantially altering Section 605. Congressional inaction has also been made easier by the willingness of Justice Department officials, local police, state legislators, and federal judges to cope with the wiretapping problem.

In recent years, Justice Department officials have been asking for less and less serious changes in Section 605, and it may well be that the legislative log jam will some day be broken by a compromise allowing use in federal courts of wiretapping evidence, provided, as in other searches and seizures, police have first obtained a warrant from a judicial official. Such a change would alter the judicial role in the wiretapping controversy, but might not diminish the importance of that role. Judges would still have to determine whether police had shown probable cause and whether the search was reasonable.

It is possible that congressional action will be spurred by a Supreme Court decision applying the full force of the *Weeks* and *Nardone* rules to state court proceedings. In 1961, the justices took advantage of an opportunity in *Mapp* v. *Ohio*[1] to overrule *Wolf* v. *Colorado,* the precedent on whose authority *Schwartz* v. *Texas* and *Irvine* v. *California* had been decided. The basis of *Schwartz,* however, was only weakened, not destroyed. The Mapp opinion stressed that it was evidence obtained by unconstitutional (not merely illegal) means that could not be used in state courts; and in *Pugach* v. *Dollinger,*[2] decided less than four months before *Mapp,* a majority of the justices then on the bench affirmed *Schwartz.* Moreover, a year after *Mapp,* the Court refused to grant certiorari to review a New York ruling upholding admission of wiretap evidence in a state trial.[3] The fate of *Schwartz* was thus left in doubt. A denial of certiorari may be based on many factors and does not necessarily indicate that the justices approve either the decision or the doctrine of the lower court. Furthermore, though *Pugach* was decided shortly before *Mapp,* its decision was announced before *Mapp* was even argued.

Perhaps most important for the future of the *Schwartz* rule and its permissive policy for state courts is whether the general civil libertarian orientation of the Warren Court will continue. In the recent past a majority of the justices has been willing to extend decisions like *Mapp* to protect individual liberty against police actions.[4] It is even possible, though less likely than an extension of the exclusionary rule, that the Court will overrule *Olmstead*.

The wiretapping conflict has been waged largely among government officials, though some private interests, such as telephone companies, labor unions, and civil liberties organizations have lobbied before Congress and the courts. More commonly, perhaps, large pressure groups play a more central role in conflicts over issues of domestic policy. Yet whether the major contestants are private citizens or government officials, the basic process remains essentially the same. Judicial rulings may settle specific pieces of litigation; alone, they seldom silence competing social demands. It is no less true that, taken by themselves, neither congressional nor administrative decisions are likely to quiet such controversies. The American system of government provides too many avenues of access to authoritative decision-making for any particular agency to say the final word on a controversial issue of significance to broad segments of public policy. Representatives of the losing interest—and they may or may not have been among the actual litigants personally involved—in one governmental forum usually have an opportunity to take their threatened cause to another governmental agency. And the loser in that forum has a similar opportunity to take his interest to another forum, and so on until the interests involved have been physically or financially exhausted, a viable compromise reached, or the problem outlived.

What judges will decide in such situations will vitally affect but not finally determine state and federal policies. Above all else, the handling of the wiretapping problem demonstrates the continuous nature of the process involved in making public policy on a live and disputed issue. Because of their authority to interpret the Constitution, acts of Congress, and executive orders, it is inevitable that the justices of the Supreme Court play an important part in that process.

Bibliographical Note

The Era of the 1920s

Among the great number of excellent books on the period 1920–1930 are: Frederick Lewis Allen, *Only Yesterday* (New York: Harper & Bros., 1931); John D. Hicks, *Republican Ascendancy: 1921-1933* (New York: Harper & Bros., 1960); William Allen White, *A Puritan in Babylon: The Story of Calvin Coolidge* (New York: Macmillan Co., 1939); and George Mowry (ed.), *The Twenties: Fords, Flappers, and Fanatics* (Englewood Cliffs, N.J.: Prentice-Hall, Inc., 1963). Among the best books on prohibition are: Peter H. Odegard, *Pressure Politics: The Story of the Anti-Saloon League* (New York: Columbia University Press, 1928) and Andrew Sinclair, *Prohibition: Era of Excess* (Boston: Little, Brown, 1962). Recent and readable is Henry Lee Moon, *How Dry We Were* (Englewood Cliffs, N.J.: Prentice-Hall, Inc., 1963). Perhaps the most damning commentary on the "noble experiment" is the final report of the Wickersham Committee, a group of distinguished people, more or less sympathetic to prohibition, appointed by President Hoover to recommend ways of strengthening law enforcement: National Commission on Law Observance and Enforcement, *Report on the Enforcement of the Prohibition Laws of the United States* (Washington, D.C.: Government Printing Office, 1931).

Wiretapping

Here again there is a huge mass of literature, including in recent years hearings conducted by the House and Senate committees on the judiciary. These hearings have taken on the status of an annual or semiannual affair and contain much valuable material. Among the other works I found most useful are: Samuel Dash, Richard F. Schwartz, and Robert Knowlton, *The Eavesdroppers* (New Brunswick, N.J.: Rutgers University Press, 1959); Alan Westin, "The Wire-Tapping Problem: An Analysis and a Legislative Proposal," 52 *Columbia Law Review* 165 (1952); David M. Helfeld, "A Study of the Justice Department Policies on Wiretapping," 9 *Lawyers Guild Review* 57 (1949); and Symposium, "The Wiretapping–Eavesdropping Problem," 44 *Minnesota Law Review* 15 (1960). Among the recent popular works are: Vance Packard, *The Naked Society* (New York: David McKay, 1964); and Myron Brenton, *The Privacy Invaders* (New York: Coward-McCann, 1964).

The Supreme Court and American Politics

Choice is even more difficult here. I would recommend: Edward S. Corwin, *The Doctrine of Judicial Review* (Princeton: Princeton University Press, 1914); J. W. Peltason, *Federal Courts in the Political Process* (New York: Random House, 1956); Robert G. McCloskey, *The American Supreme Court* (Chicago: University of Chicago Press, 1960); Alpheus T. Mason, *The Supreme Court from Taft to Warren* (Baton Rouge, La.: Louisiana State University Press, 1958); Walter F. Murphy and C. Herman Pritchett, *Courts, Judges and Politics* (New York: Random House, 1961); C. Herman Pritchett, *The American Constitution* (New York: McGraw Hill, 1959); and Walter F. Murphy, *Congress and the Court* (Chicago: University of Chicago Press, 1962).

References

Preface

1. See my book review at 16 *Journal of Legal Education* 360 (1964).

Chapter 1. Introduction

1. For a more complete discussion of the limitations on judicial power see my *Elements of Judicial Strategy* (Chicago: University of Chicago Press, 1964), Chap. 2, and Walter F. Murphy and C. Herman Pritchett, *Courts, Judges and Politics* (New York: Random House, Inc., 1961), Chaps. 7, 15–17.
2. *Marbury* v. *Madison*, 1 Cranch 137, 177 (1803).
3. J. W. Peltason, *Federal Courts in the Political Process* (New York: Random House, Inc., 1956), p. 3.

Chapter 2. Prohibition

1. Frederick Lewis Allen, *Only Yesterday* (New York: Harper & Bros., 1931), p. 275. (I have used the Bantam Books edition of 1946.)
2. Laurence F. Schmeckebier, *The Bureau of Prohibition* (Washington, D.C.: The Brookings Institution, 1929), p. 57.

3. Robert A. Dahl and Charles Lindblom, *Politics, Economics, and Welfare* (New York: Harper & Bros., 1953), p. 342.

Chapter 3. The Olmstead Gang

1. This conversation was reported in Earl Corwin's testimony at Olmstead's trial. The other conversations referred to later in this chapter were also reported at the trial. Each federal court keeps in its files a record of all trial proceedings —motions, testimony, rulings, etc.—before it. When a case is appealed to a higher court, a copy of these records—or relevant portions—is sent to the appellate tribunal. The records I have used in this book are those in the Supreme Court Library. Copies may be found in the Library of Congress and in several leading law libraries around the country.
2. *Seattle Daily Times,* Nov. 18, 1924.
3. *Ibid.,* Nov. 19, 1924.
4. *Ibid.*
5. *Ibid.,* Nov. 20, 1924.
6. *Ibid.,* Nov. 25, 1924.
7. *Ibid.,* Jan. 21, 1925.
8. *United States* v. *Olmstead,* 7 F. 2d 760, 763 (1925). The 763 means that the particular sentences quoted appear on p. 763 of vol. 7 of the second series of the Federal Reporter. See above p. 26n. for an explanation of the legal citation system.

Chapter 4. The Trial

1. *Seattle Daily Times,* Jan. 19, 1926.
2. See the biography of Vandeveer: L. S. Hawley and R. B. Potts, *Counsel for the Damned* (Philadelphia: J. B. Lippincott Co., 1953).
3. See note 1, Chap. 3, for an explanation of the trial record.
4. *Seattle Daily Times,* Jan. 31, 1926.
5. *Ibid.,* Jan. 26, 1926.
6. *Ibid.,* Feb. 21, 1926.

Chapter 5. Appeal

1. Actually, the defendants had petitioned for a "writ of error," an appellate procedure that dropped out of use in the federal courts just about the time of the Olmstead case. When such a procedure was used the party seeking review was called "the plaintiff-in-error"; the other party, "the defendant-in-error."

2. 19 F. 2d 842 (1927).

3. 19 F. 2d 850 (1927).

4. *Olmstead* v. *United States*, 19 F. 2d 842, 847 (1927).

5. *Weeks* v. *United States*, 232 U.S. 383 (1914).

6. *Olmstead* v. *United States*, 19 F. 2d 842, 850 (1927).

7. Current Supreme Court rules forbid separate supporting briefs. The reasons for requesting certiorari must be stated in the petition itself. The party who won in the lower court may file a succinct brief outlining his reasons for opposing further review of the case.

8. The petition is in the Supreme Court Library and is filed with the briefs and records in the Olmstead case.

9. 275 U.S. 557 (1927). "U.S." here refers to the United States Reports, the official edition of the opinions of the Supreme Court published by the Government Printing Office. Several private companies also publish editions of the Court's opinions. The Lawyers Cooperative Publishing Company puts out one set, known as the Lawyers' Edition and cited as "L. ed." and in its second series as "L. ed. 2d." The West Publishing Company sells another edition, known as the Supreme Court Reports and cited as "S. Ct." *The United States Law Week*, a periodical, also prints the Court's opinions; this journal is cited as "U.S. Law W." or "U.S.L.W." The citations in this book are to the official reports.

10. 276 U.S. 609, 609-10 (1928).

Chapter 6. The Taft Court

1. Gus Karger to William Howard Taft, May 25, 1921; The Papers of William Howard Taft, the Library of Congress.

2. WHT to Mabel Boardman, May 31, 1921; Taft Papers.

3. WHT to George Sutherland, July 2, 1921; The Papers of George Sutherland, the Library of Congress.

4. Holmes to Harold Laski, May 27, 1921; Mark DeWolfe Howe (ed.), *Holmes–Laski Letters* (Cambridge, Mass.: Harvard University Press, 1953), I, 339.

5. Holmes to Sir Frederick Pollock, Oct. 2, 1921; Mark DeWolfe Howe (ed.), *Holmes–Pollock Letters* (Cambridge, Mass.: Harvard University Press, 1942), II, 79.

6. WHT to Horace Taft, Oct. 6, 1921; Taft Papers.

7. WHT to each Senior Circuit Judge, Dec. 19, 1921; Taft Papers.

8. WHT to the Chief Judge of the Kentucky Court of Appeals, Feb. 4, 1922; Taft Papers.

9. WHT to Robert A. Taft, March 10, 1923; Taft Papers.

10. Quoted in Henry Pringle, *The Life and Times of William Howard Taft* (New York: Farrar & Rinehart, 1939), I, 536.

11. This is the thesis of Alpheus T. Mason's excellent study, *William Howard Taft: Chief Justice* (New York: Simon & Schuster, Inc., 1965).

12. WHT to Elihu Root, Dec. 21, 1922; Taft Papers.

13. *Osborn* v. *Bank of the United States*, 9 Wh. 738, 866 (1824). The Wh. stands for Wheaton. Until after the Civil War, Supreme Court opinions were published in volumes under the name of the official reporter of the Court. Thus the early reports are: Dallas, Cranch, Wheaton, Peters, Howard, Black, and Wallace.

14. Draft of a tribute to Edward D. White, *ca.* May 1921; Taft Papers.

15. *Lochner* v. *New York*, 198 U.S. 45, 75 (1905).

16. Max Lerner (ed.), *The Mind and Faith of Mr. Justice Holmes* (New York: Random House, 1943), p. xxxv.

17. *New State Ice Co.* v. *Liebmann*, 285 U.S. 262, 311 (1932).

18. Quoted in Alexander Bickel, *The Unpublished Opin-*

ions of Mr. Justice Brandeis (Cambridge, Mass.: The Belknap Press of Harvard University Press, 1957), p. 222.

19. Quoted in Bickel, *The Unpublished Opinions of Mr. Justice Brandeis,* p. 220.

20. Holmes to Harold Laski, Jan. 6, 1923; Howe (ed.), *Holmes–Laski Letters,* I, 469.

21. WHT to Robert A. Taft, Dec. 17, 1924; Taft Papers.

22. *Nebbia* v. *New York,* 291 U.S. 502, 556 (1934).

23. WHT to Helen Taft Manning, June 11, 1923; Taft Papers.

24. Joel F. Paschal, *Mr. Justice Sutherland: A Man against the State* (Princeton: Princeton University Press, 1951).

25. *Adkins* v. *Children's Hospital,* 261 U.S. 525, 546 (1923).

26. Stone to his sons, Jan. 7, 1938; The Papers of Harlan Fiske Stone, the Library of Congress.

27. The nearest approach to a full-scale biography of Butler is David Danelski's insightful book, *A Supreme Court Justice Is Appointed* (New York: Random House, 1964).

28. *The Malcomb Baxter, Jr.,* 277 U.S. 323 (1928); the slip opinion is filed in the Stone Papers.

29. WHT to Warren G. Harding, Dec. 4, 1922; Taft Papers.

30. WHT to Henry Taft, Jan. 16, 1923; Taft Papers.

31. Harold Laski to Holmes, July 29, 1924; Howe (ed.), *Holmes–Laski Letters,* I, 638.

32. Laski to Holmes, Aug. 26, 1925; *Holmes–Laski Letters,* I, 780.

33. "Stop Helping the Criminal," Interview with O. P. Newman, 79 *Colliers* 8 (Jan. 22, 1927).

34. Samuel D. Warren and Louis D. Brandeis, "The Right to Privacy," 4 *Harvard Law Review* 193 (1890).

35. *Debs* v. *United States,* 249 U.S. 211 (1919).

36. *Moore* v. *Dempsey,* 261 U.S. 86 (1923).

37. *Powell* v. *Alabama,* 287 U.S. 45 (1932).

38. Compare Butler's votes in *Buck* v. *Bell,* 274 U.S.

200 (1927), and *Palko* v. *Connecticut*, 302 U.S. 319 (1937), with those in *Near* v. *Minnesota*, 283 U.S. 697 (1931), and *Powell* v. *Alabama*, 287 U.S. 45 (1932).

Chapter 7. The Justices Deliberate

1. *INS* v. *AP*, 248 U.S. 215 (1918).

2. Quoted in Henry Pringle, *The Life and Times of William Howard Taft*, I, 115.

3. *Seattle Daily Times*, Feb. 21, 1928.

4. The Seattle newspapers covering the oral argument did not note his absence.

5. For a discussion of bargaining within the Court, see my *Elements of Judicial Strategy* (Chicago: University of Chicago Press, 1964), Chap. 3.

6. Quoted in David Danelski, "The Chief Justice and the Supreme Court," Ph.D. Diss., University of Chicago, 1961, p. 179.

7. The various letters and memoranda among the majority justices can be found in the Taft Papers (which are arranged chronologically) in the files for the last week of May and the first few days in June.

8. Holmes to Sir Frederick Pollock, June 20, 1928; Mark DeWolfe Howe (ed.), *Holmes–Pollock Letters*, II, 222.

9. HFS to Louis D. Brandeis, March 23, 1928; Stone Papers.

10. *Olmstead* v. *United States*, 277 U.S. 438 (1928).

Chapter 8. The Justices Speak

1. 116 U.S. 616 (1886).

2. 232 U.S. 383 (1914).

3. 96 U.S. 727 (1878).

4. 251 U.S. 385 (1920).

5. 255 U.S. 313 (1921).

6. 255 U.S. 298 (1921).

7. 267 U.S. 132 (1925).

8. 265 U.S. 57 (1924).

9. 4 Wh. 316, 407 (1819).

Chapter 9. Impact

1. WHT to Horace Taft, June 8, 1928; Taft Papers.
2. WHT to Horace Taft, June 12, 1928; *ibid.*
3. 126 *The Nation* 679 (June 20, 1928); unless otherwise noted, the remaining editorials are reprinted in 28 *Literary Digest* 10 (June 16, 1928).
4. June 6, 1928, 24:2.
5. HFS to Brandeis, June 7, 1928; Stone Papers.
6. Van Devanter to WHT, June 16, 1928; Taft Papers.
7. HFS to Brandeis, June 7, 1928; Stone Papers.
8. Van Devanter to WHT, June 25, 1928; Taft Papers.
9. U.S. House of Representatives, Subcommittee of the Committee on Appropriations, *Hearings on Department of Justice Appropriations Bill for* 1932, 71st Cong., 3rd Sess., pp. 116-17 (1930).
10. U.S. House of Representatives, Committee on Expenditures in the Executive Departments, *Hearings: Wiretapping in Law Enforcement*, 71st Cong., 3rd Sess., p. 26 (1931).
11. See reference in note 10, above, p. 2.
12. 74 *Congressional Record* 2905 (1931).
13. U.S. House of Representatives, Subcommittee of the Committee on Appropriations, *Hearings on Department of Justice Appropriations Bill for* 1933, 72nd Cong., 1st Sess., p. 253 (1932).
14. U.S. House of Representatives, *Hearings . . . for* 1934, 72nd Cong., 2nd Sess., pp. 33, 35–6 (1932).
15. *United States* v. *Nardone*, 90 F. 2d 630, 632 (1937).
16. 302 U.S. 379 (1937).
17. 308 U.S. 338 (1939).
18. See, for example, *Weiss* v. *United States*, 308 U.S. 321 (1939); *United States* v. *Polakoff*, 112 F. 2d 888 (1940); and *United States* v. *Fallon*, 112 F. 2d 894 (1940).
19. Attorney General Robert H. Jackson quoted this letter in a public statement on wiretapping, reprinted at 87 *Cong. Rec.* A1472 (1940).
20. Senate Report #1304, 76th Cong., 3rd Sess. (1940).

21. The text of the order and the accompanying press release can be found at 86 *Cong. Rec.* 1471-72 (1940).

22. Quoted in Francis Biddle, *In Brief Authority* (New York: Doubleday, 1962), p. 167. Biddle succeeded Jackson as Attorney General when Jackson was appointed to the Supreme Court.

23. Jackson to Rep. Hatton Summers, Feb. 10, 1941; U.S. House of Representatives, Committee on the Judiciary, *To Authorize Wiretapping: Hearings on H.R. 2266 and H.R.* 3099, 77th Cong., 1st Sess., p. 17 (1941).

24. Jackson to Hatton Summers, March 19, 1941; Committee on the Judiciary, *To Authorize Wiretapping . . .*, pp. 18–19.

25. Committee on the Judiciary, *To Authorize Wiretapping . . .*, p. 112.

26. Franklin D. Roosevelt to Thomas Eliot, Feb. 21, 1941; Committee on the Judiciary, *To Authorize Wiretapping . . .*, p. 257.

27. *New York Times*, Oct. 9, 1941, 4:2.

Chapter 10. Olmstead *Revisited*

1. 316 U.S. 129 (1942).

2. Murphy's notes are in his papers, now located in the Michigan Historical Collections, University of Michigan, Ann Arbor.

3. In Murphy's case files one often finds a set of directions from the justice to his clerk, then a handwritten copy of an opinion draft in his clerk's writing, then a typewritten copy with comments and changes in Murphy's handwriting, then several different printed versions, some heavily edited by Murphy, and others, which had been circulated in the Court, with suggestions from the other justices.

4. The draft is in the Stone Papers.

5. Felix Frankfurter to Frank Murphy, March 5, 1942; copies are in the Stone and Murphy Papers.

6. Felix Frankfurter to Frank Murphy, April 3, 1942; Murphy Papers.

7. 338 U.S. 25 (1949).

8. 344 U.S. 199 (1952).

9. Alan Westin, "'Bookies and Bugs' in California," in Westin (ed.), *The Uses of Power* (New York: Harcourt, Brace & World, 1962), p. 125.

10. 355 U.S. 96 (1957).

11. See the account in Westin, "'Bookies and Bugs' in California."

12. 343 U.S. 747 (1952).

13. 347 U.S. 128 (1954).

14. *Rathbun* v. *United States,* 355 U.S. 107 (1957).

15. The opinion of the trial judge is reported at 88 F. Supp. 921 (1950); reversed by the Court of Appeals, 185 F. 2d 629 (1950); certiorari denied, 342 U.S. 926 (1952). The opinion of the trial judge at a second trial is reported at 91 F. Supp. 867 (1950); reversed by the Court of Appeals, 191 F. 2d 749 (1951).

Chapter 11. Conclusion

1. 367 U.S. 643 (1961).

2. 365 U.S. 458 (1961).

3. *Dinan* v. *New York,* 371 U.S. 877 (1962).

4. See especially: *Ker* v. *California,* 374 U.S. 23 (1963); *Fahey* v. *Connecticut,* 375 U.S. 85 (1963); *Stoner* v. *California,* 376 U.S. 483 (1964); *Clinton* v. *Virginia,* 377 U.S. 158 (1964); and *Aguilar* v. *Texas,* 378 U.S. 39 (1964).

Index

STUDIES IN POLITICAL SCIENCE

Natural Resources and the Political Struggle
Norman Wengert PS 24
Federal Courts in the Political Process
Jack W. Peltason PS 25
The Study of Political Parties
Neil A. McDonald PS 26
Security and Liberty: The Problem of Native Communists
H. W. Chase PS 27
Government and Politics in Africa South of the Sahara, revised and enlarged edition
T. R. Adam PS 28
The Study of Local Politics
William H. Riker PS 29
Money and Politics
J. B. Shannon PS 30
Government and Politics in Latin America
R. A. Gomez PS 32
The Presidency: A Modern Perspective
Francis H. Heller PS 33
Communism, revised and enlarged edition
A. G. Meyer PS 34
Public Opinion and Foreign Policy
James N. Rosenau PS 35
Courts and Rights: The American Judiciary in Action
John P. Roche PS 36
The State Legislature: Politics and Practice
Malcolm E. Jewell PS 37
Contemporary Southeast Asia
Robert C. Bone, Jr. PS 38
Small City Government: Seven Cases in Decision Making
Warner E. Mills, Jr. and Harry R. Davis PS 39
The Constitution and the Court
Robert S. Hirschfield PS 40
Propaganda and Psychological Warfare
Terence H. Qualter PS 41

The Behavioral Persuasion in Politics
Heinz Eulau — PS 42

Mr. Secretary of State
Norman L. Hill — PS 43

Latin America: Political Institutions and Processes
James L. Busey — PS 44

Congress: Politics and Practice
Norman C. Thomas and Karl A. Lamb — PS 45

A Supreme Court Justice Is Appointed
David Danelski — PS 46

Africa: The Primacy of Politics
Herbert Spiro (Ed.) — PS 47

Big City Politics
Edward C. Banfield — PS 48

Marxism and Communism: Essential Readings
Robert V. Daniels (Ed.) — PS 49

Wiretapping on Trial: A Case Study in the Judicial Process
Walter F. Murphy — PS 50

The Revolution in Statecraft
Andrew M. Scott — PS 51

Judicial Review and Democracy
Howard E. Dean — PS 52

The United Nations and the Superpowers
John G. Stoessinger — PS 53

The Political Theory of American Local Government
Anwar Syed — PS 54